AN AFRICAN SON

Abewat

Ron Peterson

Wisdom
Editions

Minneapolis

FIRST EDITION MAY 2022
An African Son: Abraham Boi Watson's Perilous Journey
Copyright © 2022 by Ronald E. Peterson.
All rights reserved.

For information, write to Calumet Editions,
6800 France Avenue South, Suite 370, Edina, MN 55435

Printed in the United States of America.
10 9 8 7 6 5 4 3 2 1
ISBN: 978-1-950743-82-7

Cover and interior design: Gary Lindberg

AN AFRICAN SON

Abraham Boi Watson's Perilous Journey

Ronald E. Peterson

Wisdom
Editions

Minneapolis

Table of Contents

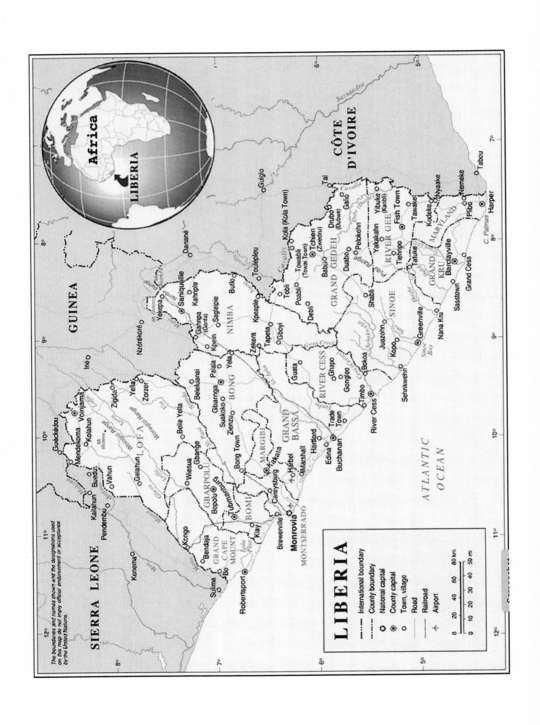

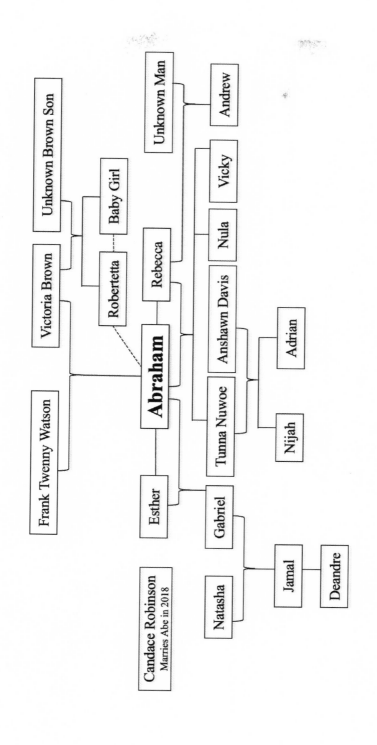

Also by Ronald E. Peterson

An Introvert Learns to Fly

Gardeners of the Universe

Author's Note

I've known Abraham Watson for over twenty-five years. We met when he joined our small multiracial church. An affable Black man with a permanent smile, he sometimes told stories about his escape during the Liberian civil war, a miraculous journey that saved his life and the lives of his family. Over the years, Abe and I worked together on a multitude of projects, learned to trust one another and became friends. Abe is my opposite, an unstoppable extrovert and ambassador for our tiny congregation, while I often revert to my true nature, a hopeless introvert. After retiring as a rather odd vice president of one of the largest corporations in the US, I traveled, explored multiple roles and started to write, first about myself (*An Introvert Learns to Fly*) and later an award-winning science fiction novel (*Gardeners of the Universe*). My life's to-do list includes writing five meaningful books—and Abe's remarkable life story needed to be told.

Abe often describes his travels across Liberia's brutal warring countryside because that is the time when everything in his life was at stake. Liberia's civil war was not an ordinary war. Overlaid on the usual greed, corruption, hatred and outrage was a complex mixture of spiritual forces. Clashing ideas from Christianity, Islam and dozens of spirit-centered tribes led to children soldiers with automatic rifles, sometimes wearing dresses, clerical robes, hospital gowns or women's wigs, their faces painted bright colors, bragging about killing and eating their victims' hearts.[1]

During extensive interviews with Abe and his family, I learned that even his peaceful years are fascinating and instructive. Growing up as a member of the Kpelle (pronounced Pella) tribe made his life difficult from its beginning. Liberians from the capital of Monrovia considered tribal members third-class, uncivilized and close to slaves. How he managed to become an electrician and employee of the Voice of America is remarkable. His family's journey from Liberia to the Ivory Coast (now called the Côte d'Ivoire), then to frigid Fargo/Moorhead, and finally Minneapolis/St. Paul is enlightening.

Racism and prejudice have traveled with him throughout this journey. How he has dealt with hidden and open racial hatred while still surviving and thriving is his message to our hearts.

June 17, 1990

Over one hundred armed rebels blasted through the Voice of America's (VOA) inner fence around 9:00 p.m. Abe was with his family at the separate VOA housing area a mile away, but they heard the gunfire and explosions. Abe had only recently managed to get his family out of danger from the besieged city of Kakata, about twelve miles away. For a precious few weeks, they had felt safe.

"Hearing the explosions, I knew the rebels had finally invaded the facility and were probably arresting my co-workers and friends. I had worried about this moment," Abe said. *Should I turn myself in to the rebels or stay with the family?* I asked myself. If we were arrested later, the rebels would assume we were hiding and might kill us all. Lives were very cheap to them. My eight-year-old daughter Nuwoe and wife, Rebecca, begged me to stay. It was the most painful decision of my life. To protect my family, I felt I had to turn myself in. Nuwoe had her arms wrapped around my leg as I broke away.

"I walked the forest road alone toward the transmitter area in an African blackness—no moon, no stars and no lights anywhere. Just staying on the road in the deep forest was difficult.

I imagined that I was probably committing suicide and repeatedly prayed the Lord's Prayer as I walked.

"Close to the VOA operations area, I saw that all the lights had been shot out. Holding my empty hands high, I walked haltingly among the rebels, most with flashlights and guns. I kept my head down until I spotted someone who seemed to be in charge and reported to him. The rebel leader asked my name and where I was from, and I was officially arrested and shoved into a van, where I found three other VOA workers. We were taken four or five miles away to what they called the general's house, a huge house where a wealthy man named Albert White had lived. They had killed him, and a rebel general claimed the house.

"That's what they did everywhere—came into a town, killed everyone and claimed that it was theirs. Sometimes they painted their names on the houses to prove they were under new ownership.

"At the general's house, I had to sign a list by the light of a lantern. There were at least a hundred guards and soldiers in the area. I was shoved into a basement where I found most of the other VOA workers were already imprisoned, along with many people I didn't know. Near 11:00 p.m., with no alternatives, most of the fifty exhausted prisoners fell asleep on the concrete floor or leaning against a wall. I couldn't sleep for a long time, but others were snoring.

"We were all startled early the next morning when a military woman barged in and said to our guards, 'Why are you keeping them here? Don't you know this is where they take people into the bush to kill them? We might need some of them. Get them out of here.'

"We were all marched outside at gunpoint. Another soldier, a commander, we were told, strode up to us around 7:00 a.m., waving an AK-47 with one arm and an open bottle of liquor with the other. He said, 'Form a line. Do you see this Schnapps? I'm going behind the house to drink it, and when I return, someone is going to fall.' At that point we all panicked. I considered running but there was really no way out since we were completely surrounded by armed rebels.

"When the commander returned, he fired a round over our heads, drew a line on the ground and started dividing us by tribe.

He shouted at me, 'What's your name, and where are you from?' It wasn't clear why the commander wanted to know which tribes we were from, but I said Kpelle and stayed on his side of the line. I kept my head up and smiled as much as possible. The man next to me looked terrified and hung his head low, hiding his face. A rebel slapped the butt end of an AK-47 across his head.

"It was hot that morning, and they forced us to stand the whole time—at least five rifles were pointed at us.

"Eventually, that commander was told that he was needed on the battlefield near Monrovia, and another rebel took charge. The new guy started calling out names, including mine, and locked a group of us into a van. The van bounced violently as we headed off somewhere. It was burning hot in there. Everyone was sweating and certain we were being hauled off to the bush to be eliminated."

Chapter 1—Loaning Out Children

Abe's Family

Like so many in Liberia, Abe was born into a family of subsistence farmers. In some ways, the word subsistence cuts much deeper and wider. It was actually subsistence *living*, especially for the majority of Indigenous Liberians, like Abe's family.

It was not unusual for such poor parents to loan or even transfer their children to others. Sending Indigenous children to live with a more prosperous family reduced the expense of raising the child and had the potential for enriching the child's life. The parents were generally told the child would be well-cared-for and receive a better education than the family could provide. For some, it was also an opportunity to be officially "civilized" by acquiring an American-sounding name. But for most such children, it meant a life of near-slavery. Their playtime was lost. In a sense, their childhood was stolen.

Abe was born on February 7, 1953, in Careysburg, about twenty-five miles northeast of the Liberian capital, Monrovia. Both his parents, Frank and Victoria, had been loaned out as they grew up.

Abe's father's Indigenous name was Bena Twenny. He acquired the name Frank Twenny Watson when he was raised by an American Baptist missionary, Francis B. Watson, in a town called Frank Town. The children who came to her mission from throughout Liberia all took the name Watson before leaving. She was responsible for roughly a dozen children at one time, including their general education and instruction in Christianity. Frank grew up in the mission orphanage and was treated very well by Francis Watson. In fact, when she finally returned to the US, she had a plan to smuggle several of the children, including Frank, out of Liberia and officially adopt them. She wasn't able to pull that off. Much later, when she was a very old woman, she went back to Liberia for a visit and stayed with Frank Watson and his family.

Similarly, Abe's mother, Victoria, was about twelve when she was loaned to the District Commissioner by her parents. The District Commissioner was a very important position. Before the general availability of cars, people with that title would be carried by male slaves in a hammock-like sling between towns, as one sees in old movies.

Details about her biological family are unknown, but as an Indigenous girl, Victoria (nicknamed Vic) hadn't attended school before being loaned out. The commissioner's family promised that she would receive a good education. In fact, she received none and was treated like a maid. Within a few years, Victoria gave birth to a girl who soon died (Baby Girl), then a daughter named Robertetta (pronounced Robert-etta). Both were fathered by one of the commissioner's sons. Victoria acquired the last name Brown from the family where she was captive.

No one knows how Victoria and Frank met. It's possible he did some carpentry work for the Brown family and got to know her then, but it is mostly a mystery. They were married around 1950, and Victoria and Robertetta were finally able to leave the Brown family.

Abe's mother Victoria. (Watson family photo)

Abraham Boi Watson's name had a very common structure. The western name Watson indicated that his family was educated. The first name, Abraham, was from the Bible, indicating that he was Christian. The middle name, Boi, was from the tribal language and meant "active." As a baby, Abe thrashed his arms and legs when he was awake. Abe was about sixteen years younger than Robertetta.

Frank worked from time to time as a carpenter and a jailer, but mostly, like the majority of the Kpelle tribe, as a farmer. They lived in a house on a hill near the busy Monrovia-Kakata highway in Careysburg. Frank built that house himself by erecting and weaving support sticks and covering the outside with mud. It had a palm-leaf-thatched roof, a dirt floor and a cooking area out back.

The internal space was divided into four bedrooms—one for the parents, one for Abe, another for Robertetta and a fourth for guests. There was no general sitting area, like a living room, inside. Due to the incessant Liberia heat, everyone gathered out front to talk and watch the traffic pass by. They didn't have electricity when Abe was young, so at night they would light lamps or lanterns. Cooking and drinking water was available using buckets from a well they had dug out back. There also was a large deep well in town that everyone shared.

Careysburg, a middle-size town of about thirty thousand people, was first settled in 1859 by freed North American slaves, the Americo-Liberians. The city was named for the Reverend Lott Carey.[2] Carey led the first Baptist missionaries to Africa from the United States in 1821. His pioneering missionary team settled in Liberia, where they founded the first Baptist church in Monrovia. Abe grew up among a mixture of the wealthier Americo-Liberian children and many Indigenous Tribal children like himself.

The main highway in Careysburg acted as an open-air market, where families would set up tables near their houses to sell food and goods to drivers. Signs were hung out by the road so travelers would know what was being sold that day. Sometimes drivers would just honk, and someone had to run out to see what they wanted. People from Monrovia especially liked to buy things they couldn't get in town, like fresh bananas, pine nuts, etc. Robertetta made beautiful quilts that she sold. The Watson family members would sit outside all day to sell rice, firewood, grapefruit, tangerines and mangoes from trees they had planted in the back of their house, as well as some vegetables like cassava. Competition came from other families as well as two Lebanese wholesale markets nearby that sold both regional and imported items, sometimes undercutting prices and annoying the locals. The Lebanese had been in Liberia for over one hundred years, and many more moved to Liberia during the 1975–1990 Lebanon civil war.

During Abraham's early years, everyone just called him Boi. His chores were helping on the farm, gathering firewood and "mowing" the tall grasses in their yard. Mowing was done by hacking the ground with a hoe, or machete, often digging up the grass. "Sometimes a loose gravel chunk would shoot out and hit your leg," Abe said.

Abe remembers, "After sunset, we would sit out, young friends together and the older folks in a separate group, with lanterns, lamps or the light of the fire. Friends might bring some food to share. We listened to music from a radio, and some sang along—me, not so much. A few kids made copies of the radio songs and sold the tapes. Copyright laws were essentially nonexistent there. Mostly, everyone would talk or play Lido, a board game. We younger boys had kind of a gang, but a completely non-violent one; mostly, we were just friends. It might be 75 degrees in the evening, but after the terrible heat of the day, it seemed chilly, and people would wear jackets. Occasionally, the ocean breeze would cool it off more. The front porch had a roof that extended and kept us dry during the rainy season. Liberia has three seasons, Rainy (June to October), Dry (November to March) and Mid-Dry (March to May).

"Early most mornings, we walked to the creek to bathe because getting water from the well was too slow. Going in the river was cold, but it sure woke us up. I remember the morning steam or fog floating over the river. Then we would have some rice dish for breakfast. My mom made sure we were always well fed—traditional food. I have always been thin, though I am not sure why, since we always ate a lot.

"During the rainy season, I had to go to school in the morning and work on the farm after school. If we got wet, which happened a lot, we changed clothes at home or sat by a fire to dry off. But, if it rained on the way to school and we got soaked, we just had to sit in class as we dried off. Sometimes we tried holding a dried

palm leaf over our heads in the rain like an umbrella, but that
didn't work well, especially on windy days."

A Watson relative selling cold water packets along the Monrovia-Kakata highway today—not greatly different from Abe's
boyhood. (Watson family photo).

Frank spoke Kpelle, his tribal language, as well as English and some
words and phrases in other Liberian native tongues. Lessons in school
were taught in English, and around the house, everyone spoke English
unless a traditional guest was present. Abe can still speak Kpelle.

They would cook and eat outdoors in the back of the house.
Most often, the food consisted of a rice base with vegetables, potatoes,
cassava, eddoes, gravy and peppers (habaneros or cayenne) mixed in.
Food was cooked in a pot on a rock over the fire. Several rocks would
be used with a metal mesh on top for large meals. The children drank
powdered Carnation milk mixed with water. If the family didn't have
milk, the children drank ground-up dried plantain mixed with water.

The Watson's often raised chickens and occasionally pigs. If people wanted cow or deer meat, they could walk down the highway and buy dried meat hanging from a post. Often, any meat in the area was fair game. "Once, we all got sick after eating some roasted groundhog that had been caught. I don't know what happened—maybe they didn't cook it long enough. I remember that felt really bad."

Dinner at the Watson house was often rice with additions from a soup bowl. The side soup was often a sweet/hot mixture called toborgee that was poured over the rice. The soup had a red palm oil base, with additions of vegetables, beans, and sometimes shrimp, crab, pork or dried fish.
(Watson family photo).

The Watson's used traditional medicines. If one's stomach hurt, Victoria would grind up bitter leaves and boil them. "Just one cup," Abe said, "would clean your system in the morning. When someone suffered from headaches from the heat, Mom had a traditional medicine to rub on your forehead. I once broke my ankle severely playing soccer. Mom snapped the bone in place and wrapped my leg with warm leaves that she had boiled. She pulled these down my ankle toward my toes, straightening out the break. Two months later, I was out playing soccer again.

"Another time, she said she had been studying a voodoo lady who had just pulled five butterflies (probably invisible) out of the ear of a person with a terrible headache. It had cured him. By then, I had learned science at school, and I told her that I didn't believe in voodoo, even if some tribal medicines actually worked.

One affliction where traditional medicines failed was malaria, a disease transmitted by bites from infected mosquitoes. The Watsons always used bed nets to keep the mosquitoes away while sleeping, but sometimes the incessant buzzing would keep them awake, and they were forced to close the windows and slap wet towels at the bugs. The nets didn't stop recurring bouts of malaria for all the family members.

Malaria's general symptoms are breathing distress, shaking chills, high fever, sweating, headache and nausea. In severe cases, people became jaundiced and vital organs were damaged. Abe remembers his experiences, "When it was 115°F, you would still feel cold and weak. During my regular bouts that could last a week, I could only eat oranges or soup. We used to take chloroquine, but if you were allergic, as I was, it would eat the crap out of you. Your skin would itch everywhere, even under your hair and the bottom of your feet." For Abe, the symptoms finally began to fade when he reached his forties. But, in a sense, malaria has sapped the strength and development of the African continent for centuries and continues to plague many countries.

Work stopped on Saturdays and Sundays. Saturdays were days of recovery from the hard work on the farm during the week. Sometimes dances or parties were held in the evening. Going to church was the only activity allowed on Sundays. No chores were allowed, not even washing clothes.

There were three churches in Careysburg, a Methodist one at the top of the hill, a Baptist one halfway down, and a Presbyterian church in the valley. Each Sunday, the Watson family walked to the Baptist church, about one-and-a-half miles away. Christian music was and still is popular in Liberia, with hymns sung a cappella in the traditional African style. "We didn't dance in the aisles as they do in some US churches, but we did sway back and forth in our chairs in time with the music. People would shout back at the preacher, saying, 'Amen' or 'Preach it, brother,' when they felt like it.

"Almost every day, friends or relatives would visit," Abe remembers. "That is just how it was in Liberia. You didn't have to tell someone you would be visiting; it was expected and happened all the time. People looked out for one another. There was a strong sense of the local community. All kinds of people visited our house, Indigenous people, Congo people, relatives and friends. Congo people, also called Americo-Liberians, were families whose relatives had once lived in America. They were people who didn't know any of the tribal languages. When too many people wanted to sleep over in the guest bedroom, Robertetta and I were kicked out of our rooms."

School (Pre-K to Third Grade)

Abe started pre-K and kindergarten on a neighbor's porch. He remembers liking the teacher because she let the kids go out and play in the mud for recess. Abe went without shoes at first but later wore shoes made from innertubes with straps cut for the tops. He wore those rubber sandals for several years until the bottoms wore through. "At school, people called me Abe, but at home, I was still Boi."

Abe began first grade at age seven at an official government school, Careysburg Public School, a free school about one-and-a-half miles away from home. Classes started at 7:30 a.m. and were done by noon. Each day would start by saluting the Liberian flag, singing the school song (which Abe still remembers) and a prayer.

"The teachers would line you up to be sure you looked good." Shirts needed to be tucked in, hair combed and fingernails were checked. The school had a long hall with many classrooms. "We had desks with side arms and a place for books, and there were about fifteen students in each classroom. I loved the math and English lessons.

"I had both Indigenous and Congo friends. It was easy to tell who the tribal kids were by their shoes. We all wore the same school uniform, but Congo kids teased me about my rubber slippers. Sometimes they called me country boy, which was a pretty derogatory name. It was like calling someone a heathen or a pagan. I might just say back, 'Hey Congo boy, you don't even know the tribal languages of this country. You are lost.' Basically, I treated all the kids based on how they were as an individual, how they treated me, good or bad.

"My Godparents were Congo people, and I was very friendly with them and their children. Some of the Congo kids at school were very arrogant, but most were okay. If a student acted up or was disrespectful toward the teacher, they might get a spanking right in front of the class. Then they would get another from their parents at home."

Both Frank and Victoria had lived with people who were wealthier, and they wanted Abe to have some of those advantages. They didn't know how to make that happen. They just wanted Abe to be strong, educated and independent.

In particular, they encouraged him to learn all his school lessons. "If I didn't go to school, father would give me a butt whipping," Abe remembers. "So I hardly ever missed. Father tried to be friendly with the teachers and said, 'If that boy gives you any trouble, let me know.' Mother was the same. Once, she spanked me and said, 'You know why I am doing this? I want you to grow up to be a very good man.' They gave me a sense of how to work for myself."

Typical Liberian classroom. (Watson family photo)

At one point, they talked about Abe becoming a tailor with a sewing machine, but Abe wasn't sure about that plan. "I didn't want to sit in one place all day long, so I didn't think much of that idea. I didn't know what I wanted to be, but it wasn't a tailor."

Before Abe started third grade, when he was about nine years old, one of the family's guava buyers, Mr. Dunbar, who often stopped by to talk to Frank, said, "I can help your child go to a better school." The man was a public works employee who traveled from Kakata to Monrovia each day. "I would like Abe to stay with me," he said, "and help around our house. I'll pay for his uniform and clothes and help him get into the government school in Kakata. The change would be good for him." There were church-run schools in Kakata but only one well-known government school, Lango Lippaye. Like all government grade schools, the new school was nominally free, but the man knew that the cost of books and uniforms might be too much for Abe's family. Frank, who himself had grown up away from his family when he was sent to live with a missionary, saw it as a good opportunity for Abe to see some new things and also a help for the family's finances. Abe, himself, was excited about the opportunity to go to a new place and learn at a better school.

So Abe left to live in Kakata with the guava buyer, staying with him and his wife. Unfortunately, the promised education became secondary to doing chores for the Dunbars. "The wife was very hostile toward me," Abe said, "too hostile. Before I went to school each day, I had to clean their dog Bill's mess and generally take care of the house. The wife would sit there with her legs crossed, smoking and staring at me, watching my every move."

With the travel time to school, he was often late for class and had to sit on the bad-boys' bench. But Lango Lippaye Afternoon School was a good school. After classes, Abe was expected to cook. When he cooked rice, he was only given the burnt crust. They fed good rice to the dog. Sometimes Mr. Dunbar would ask Abe if he was okay and slip him a little extra food. But he never heard the man argue with his wife. "She was tough," Abe said. One time, the woman started yelling at Abe, saying he hadn't cleaned the frying pan, but Abe had, so he argued back. She hit him on the head with the frying pan. He told Mr. Dunbar about it, but he didn't help at all. "Basically, they treated me like a slave."

One day, after about four months, he got so angry that he ran away. He walked four or five miles along the main Monrovia-Kakata highway, stood by a house and stopped a taxi. "I wanted them to think I lived in the house. He yelled, 'I'm going to Careysburg,' and they gave me a ride the rest of the way."

He was dropped off at Frank's carpenter shop—a worktable, saws and tools —close to the family house. But Frank and Victoria were not happy to see him. "I explained everything to them, but they thought I was lying."

Later, Mr. Dunbar stopped again at our home and explained that everything was okay and that he didn't know why Abe had run away. "That tough lady had the man in her total control," Abe said. He was forced to go back. Another boy was also there for a while, but he soon ran off. "After another month there, I told the man that she was slapping me and that I couldn't stand it. Finally, luckily, he took me home to my parents, who let me remain."

To understand Abraham's life and the world in which he grew up, and how parents could so easily send their Indigenous children off to live with another family, it is essential to know the history of Liberia and the deep reality they were responding to.

Chapter 2—Six Hundred Years Earlier

Liberia before 1821

It is believed that the Indigenous people living in modern-day Liberia migrated there, beginning in the twelfth century, from northern and eastern Africa, forming several dozen tribes. Abe's Kpelle tribe, the largest, came mostly from the area known today as Sudan. What could cause a massive number of people to migrate almost three thousand miles, often fighting throughout the journey to displace the existing populations? For those in the sub-Saharan area, where periodic droughts occur, rumors of a place with nine months of rain each year, like modern Liberia, might have sounded like a utopia, which lured them to the west.

After decades of unrecorded skirmishes, the migrants settled into relatively peaceful separate areas, each with its own language dialect, customs and spiritual practices. Some of the original groupings were tiny, just related paternalistic families. The tribes used four broad language families, Mande, Kru, Gola and Mel, with over twenty variations, like Kpelle.

One of the peoples partly displaced were the Mandingos, also known as the Malinke, an Islamic remnant of the once-dominant Mali Empire, who remained scattered among the new arrivals and who played an important role in Abraham's story. They were tradespeople who spoke Mande and congregated in the towns. A quiet stability spread across the area that lasted for centuries—until the Europeans arrived.

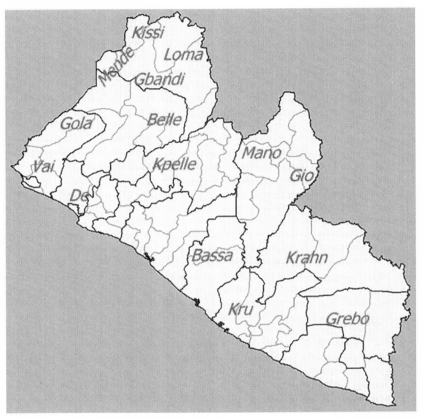

Liberian tribal areas. Abraham lived in the Kpelle area. (Creative Commons License)

The area was first reached by European explorers, the Portuguese, in 1462, and the tribes began trading their melegueta pepper, also known as the grain of paradise. Melegueta, a tiny very hot pepper, was a valuable spice. The area soon became known as the grain coast.

The abduction of African people for use as slaves in the Americas began at almost the same time. A region known as the slave coast developed south and east of Liberia, near today's Benin, Ghana, Nigeria, Angola and Congo, where more than twelve million people were snatched against their will.[3] This subjugation did not begin due to racial hatreds or national interests, but rather by acts of corporations eager for profit while indifferent toward humans with darker skin. A triangular system arose, with arms and textiles going from Europe to Africa, slaves from Africa to the Americas, and sugar and coffee going from the Americas to Europe.

Hundreds of Africans were packed tightly belowdecks in unsanitary conditions during voyages of about five thousand miles. They were typically chained together, with ceilings so low they couldn't sit upright—for months. Roughly 20 percent of the Africans aboard ship died on the voyage. (Licensed Getty image 2075989050)

Although slavery had existed throughout the world from ancient times, the abduction of African Blacks, their transport across the ocean, and their new lives in the Americas were particularly brutal and costly in terms of human life. Over the years, only 2 percent of the slave trade originated from Liberia. But the repercussions of that trade still influence the lives and culture of Liberians and other West Africans today.

In Africa, the slave trade had terrible effects on the culture by encouraging greedy warlords and creating lawlessness and violence. Clans attacked one another to capture their rivals and trade them for European goods and arms. The abductions crept deep into the African interior. Agriculture and economic development became impossible with the fighting and depopulation. Childbearing-age women and young men disappeared, leaving the elderly and disabled—those least able to contribute to economic progress.

Most of the early slave ships docked in the Caribbean Islands. The first slaves arrived in what is now the US at the Jamestown colony in 1619.[4] Demand for slave labor rose sharply in the 1600s and was legal in all the US colonies. The slave trade peaked around 1780, but became less acceptable in northern states, mostly for moral and religious reasons. Pennsylvania became the first state in the nation to officially free its slaves with the adoption of the Gradual Abolition Act of 1780, and other northern states soon followed. In 1808, importing new slaves became officially illegal throughout the US, but the trade continued in the South, with eighty thousand still arriving each year during the early 1800s.

As is well known, the treatment of slaves in the US varied, sometimes fair but often brutal, depending on the whims of their "master." By the time of the Civil War, most slaves had been in the US for three, four or five generations. The most terrifying aspect of their treatment in America during that long period was the buying and selling of individuals with the resulting destruction of many families.

As with all migrations or immigrations, by the third generation, the memory of the "old country" and its traditions began to fade. Just as today's young Americans can hardly conceive of a time before smartphones, some transplanted Africans began to feel that pain and mistreatment were normal, however much they hated it. It was their new reality.

Part of that reality was Christian slavery.[5] How and why did Christianity, seemingly built on spiritual emancipation and equality, give its blessing to African slavery in the Americas? Could slaves become Christians? If so, did their conversion lead to freedom? If not, then how could perpetual enslavement be justified? A type of perverted Christianity evolved that still exists in parts of the US South, with great emphasis on conversion and baptism throughout the world, but with muted resolve toward education, support or freedom for such baptized people—or even considering them as equals.

Return of Blacks to Africa

As the abolitionist movement grew in northern states, free Blacks there still suffered greatly from legal and economic discrimination. Various philosophical and religious condemnations of slavery, especially by Quakers, were published. Many, including Thomas Jefferson, who owned slaves, thought that returning free Blacks to Africa would lead to better lives.

Around 1800 some abolitionists, including distinguished Black shipbuilder Paul Cuffe, developed plans for Blacks to return to their African homeland, despite many having lived in the United States for generations.[6] The first ship, the *Elizabeth*, departed New York on February 6, 1820, for West Africa carrying eighty-six "settlers." Ships began to regularly carry free Blacks back to areas near current-day Monrovia. These were generally organized by the American Colonization Society (ACS), whose notable members included Thomas Buchanan, Thomas Jefferson, James Monroe, Abraham Lincoln, James Madison, Daniel Webster, John Marshall and Francis Scott Key. All were white, and most were slaveholders.

The small number of freed slaves who initially settled in Africa faced brutal conditions. Suffering from lack of food, disease and poor housing, the attrition of the colonists was terrible. Of the 4,571 emigrants who arrived in Liberia from 1820 to 1843, only 1,819 survived.[7] They were often attacked by Indigenous groups like the Mandingo tribe. But they slowly gained a secure footing through bribes, threats of force and sometimes warfare.

Soon more colonists arrived from five US states and took residence in Liberia. The African American colonists became known as Americo-Liberians, or sometimes Congo people. The American Colonization Society encouraged Liberia to proclaim its independence when it could no longer support the migration financially. On July 26, 1847, Liberia declared itself a (free) sovereign nation.[8] This was before the rest of Africa became mostly European colonies and well before they too would break the colonial bonds and achieve independence.

Americo-Liberian Rule (1847–1980)

Between 1847 and 1980, Liberia was dominated by a small minority of Black colonists from the US and their descendants. As they gained power, they transplanted their painful realities from America, which they had learned to think of as normal, to their new home in Liberia. They built a society similar to that in the US, a caste system, but now with themselves playing the role of slaveholders. Their homes and churches mirrored those they knew in the US.[9] They married within their group, built plantations and businesses, and became wealthy. They believed in the religious superiority of Protestant Christianity over tribal beliefs in the spirituality of nature—animism. The Americo-Liberians maintained overwhelming political power through many changes in leadership by not allowing the Indigenous people to vote. Although the Americo-Liberians never constituted more than 5 percent of the population of Liberia, they controlled the key resources that allowed them to enslave the native peoples and limit their access to the harbors and seas, and modern technical skills, literacy, higher education, and valuable relationships with other governments. Many received financial support from friends and relatives in the US.

Growing up, Abraham liked to talk to the older people who told stories about those times—some of which had been passed down through several generations. The tales were about how the Americo-Liberians stole their traditional land and possessions and how unfair it all was. When violence became part of the takeover, the battles were often between machetes and arrows on the traditional side and modern guns on the other. Medications, ground from special plants, were all the Indigenous people had, while Congo people (the Americo-Liberians) had Western medicines and hospitals. They all were forced to learn English and began to forget their native tongues. To this day, the Indigenous peoples' long mistreatment has not been forgotten.

After 1847, the Americo-Liberians drew boundaries for the sixteen official counties, each with an appointed leader connecting the region to the central government. This federal control, adopted from the US system, often clashed with the traditional powers, the elders and spiritual mediums. Tribal leaders believed that unseen spirits (not totally unlike Christianity or Islam) controlled their fates. Indigenous people believed those powers could be found in animals, plants, rocks and nature in general. Spiritual leaders, especially when wearing a wooden mask, were thought to, temporarily at least, embody those spirits and hence had tremendous influence over events, arguments and the future. With the Americo-Liberians in charge, local governors tied to the central government imposed a harsh new authority and began making all the important decisions.[10]

Throughout their dominance, the Americo-Liberians verbally expressed belief in "racial equality." This meant that all residents of Liberia had the potential to become "civilized," but only through

Western-style education and conversion to Christianity.[11] These social structures and strictures had a profound influence on Abraham's parents and then on Abraham as he grew up in an Indigenous family, leading to the "loaning out your children" phenomenon described earlier.

Through the many years of America-Liberian rule, from the day it became a sovereign nation in 1847 until 1980, Liberia's connection with the US varied wildly. Before Abraham Lincoln and the Thirteenth Amendment, Liberia wasn't even allowed to send a Black ambassador to the US.

During the "Scramble for Africa" in the late nineteenth century, European nations competed to expand their political empires and achieve a commercial advantage.[12] In Africa, limited competition and abundant raw materials like ivory, rubber, palm oil, cocoa, diamonds, tea and tin motivated that imperialism. During this period, the US protected Liberia from encroachment by the European powers.

Internally, the country continued to endure numerous uprisings by Indigenous tribes and political upheaval among several parties. Despite the turmoil, the wealthy and powerful True Whigs remained the dominant America-Liberian party through most of the period. In some ways, as the only West African country with Black leaders, Liberia was a model for the surrounding nations largely under colonial domination. This was a point of pride and helped the True Whig party continue its control for decades.

During World War I, the presence and protection of the United States Navy patrolling the water off the West African coast prevented European military threats to the Liberian territory and its independence. In the 1920s, the country began encouraging the exploitation of its natural resources. The rubber industry, specifically the Firestone Company, soon dominated the economy and created over twenty-five thousand jobs in a population under one million. This became even more important during World War II, when US allies needed rubber for the war effort.[13] Liberia allowed the US to use its territory as a bridgehead for transport of soldiers and war supplies and to construct military bases, airports, its largest port (Freeport of Monrovia), and thousands of miles of roads to the interior. These developments, paid for by the US, were mutually valuable, providing jobs and infrastructure useful to both countries. Many of the personnel who passed through Liberia during the war were African American soldiers being deployed into military service in Europe.

William Tubman became president of Liberia in 1944 (he had no connection to Harriet Tubman, famous for the underground railroad). Liberia's economy continued to rapidly grow after the war through US investments in facilities like the Voice of America compound, where Abraham later worked. But it was not a stable era. The new wealth was going predominately to the Americo-Liberians, and resentment grew among the majority tribal people. In 1951, social tensions forced President Tubman to make economic concessions and give the Indigenous Liberians the right to vote for the first time.

Abe grew up during the William Tubman presidency. During Tubman's long leadership from 1944 to his death in 1971, Liberia was controlled by an overbearing political patronage system, where personal relationships drove major decisions and even small ones (like business disputes and even marriages). Liberia had the second-highest rate of economic growth in the world during his reign, and by 1971 it had the largest mercantile fleet, the largest rubber industry, and was the third-largest exporter of iron ore.[14] Though Tubman is sometimes regarded as the "Father of modern Liberia," others saw him as an ignorant, although eloquent, dictator and would-be king.

The Watson family was quite aware of national and local news through newspapers and a battery-powered radio. They knew that corruption was present at all levels in Liberia, both national and local. Abe said, "We all understood that poor people like us paid the highest tax rates. Two sets of books were kept, one for the auditors and another, the real one, for the local chief minister who pocketed the extra.

While Abe was just a small boy, Tubman heard that the men of Careysburg were complaining about his policies. Tubman soon sent national soldiers into the town, arresting many. Abe's father, Frank, along with others, fled to the forests and stayed there for about two months. Wives had to sneak into the woods, as far as two miles to the hiding places, bringing food to their men. Eventually, the soldiers left, and the prisoners were freed.

Abe said, "I remember how Tubman wasted money building a zoo near his house just because his daughter wanted one and named it after her. It was all so corrupt."

Chapter 3—Growing Up in Liberia

Farm and School

Having escaped servitude with the Dunbars (the guava buyer and his wife), nine-year-old Abe was back home with his family in Careysburg and was expected to help on the farm. Because he left before the end of the school year from Lango Lippaye, he couldn't complete third grade. But at the hometown school, the teachers soon saw that he knew all the materials, so he was promoted directly to the fifth grade. "So, I didn't really waste any time, and my parents were very happy." He made sure he never missed a day of school. The family couldn't afford books, but he took notes, read all his friend's books and studied hard. "I was an A student! I learned addition, subtraction, multiplication and fractions that year and read well by then. In reading class, if you missed one word while reading aloud, you got a whap. So, I studied.

"I was a country boy who was easily overlooked. Teachers had well-to-do students who could barely pass a test, but they knew their parents were important, so they passed them to the next grade. One great motivator was the bullies who called me 'country boy' and teased me about my family and my clothes. I would say, 'Yeah, but I get better grades than you.' Some got mad at me, and we got into physical fights. Once a bigger boy attacked me, and I hit back with my fist. He was bleeding. I told my father that I had to take revenge, and he was proud of me. It just made me study harder after that."

School was held from November to July, the dryer months, with a few breaks for holidays. Christmas was a national holiday. Thanksgiving (a leftover from the Americo-Liberian time in America) was celebrated by relatives and friends getting together and sharing food.

"At school, I had both Tribal and Congo kids as friends. I didn't care about their background if they were friendly. Some of the Congo kids had lighter skin, which I ignored, although some of the Congo families did care about skin shade. They wore nicer clothes, but I only noticed if they smiled and were friendly and nice to me."

Like other family members, Abe was expected to head out to the farm every afternoon after school. Each year, the Watsons cleared a new farm area in a wooded area, away from any houses. Land ownership records were spotty. They moved "their" farmland, not because the owner showed up, but rather because the soil would give out after a year or two. Abe said, "The farms were as far as two miles away from our house and could only be reached on narrow footpaths."

Three-quarters of Liberia's land is made up of latosol, a rich but thin reddish soil. Its nutrients leach away quickly during the summer rains. While suitable for timber production, without leaf litter, latosol quickly loses its fertility. The Watsons sometimes would plant sugar cane or cassava in an old plot to try to get a second-year output. But without fertilizer, they had to start over each year for the rice crop.

Near their house, they grew corn, tomatoes, peppers, cucumbers and other vegetables and also had fruit trees (tangerines, oranges and mangoes). However, the main crop was rice. Growing rice was immensely difficult work. That region of central Liberia gets lots of rain, enough for growing rice, and almost 70 percent of Liberia's population grows rice. Everyone in the family was expected to help. Abe would get up early to fetch firewood and water before school, and after school, he would join the others in the rice field.

They cleared about four acres of the new farm area every year during the hot, dry February season—always by hand. First, both men and women hacked the brush down under trees with machetes. Then they let the brush dry and waited for a windy day. They started burning upwind, always with people watching to make sure the fire wouldn't spread too far. After the burn, they cut the trees down with axes and machetes and salvaged the limbs and sticks used to build fences.

The fencing was especially tough work, and only men took on the challenge. Solid posts were sunk every six feet, and then strong wood pieces that spanned the spaces between the posts were tied together with cords made from vines. Next, hundreds of vertical sticks, about six feet long, were leaned against the support boards, sloping away from the farm area. The sticks were set very close, inches apart around the whole field, so animals couldn't get through.

There weren't any dangerous animals in the area. Poisonous snakes would quickly glide away, and any mongoose would run from a human. Monkeys stole bananas, but they just sat in trees eating them and staring at people. A few fence sections were left open with animal traps in the openings (booby traps). Groundhogs and rabbits could be captured that way to supplement the meat supply.

Clearing the new farm area was a community undertaking. Many neighbors would help and then share in some of the output. For example, neighbors might take some of the cut tree parts for firewood. "We helped one another," Abe said.

Planting was largely done by women. A whole crew of friends would gather on a weekday to walk the new field, tossing rice mixed with a few other vegetable seeds on the surface. Women and children would then form a long line on their hands and knees and, using small hoes, hand scoops or shovels, they worked their way across the field all day, covering the seeds with soil.

The families usually took April off before the May rains began. Plants grow quickly in Liberia. Its tropical climate, high temperatures (the year-round average is 80°F), high relative humidity and heavy rainfall from May to October were perfect for rice crops. Abe said, "During the rainy months, we kept working, pulling weeds and chasing the birds when the crops started to appear. I used a sling and rocks to chase them away. We harvested and sold the other vegetable crops when they were ready, including corn, tomatoes, okra and cucumbers."

To harvest the rice, women cut the stalks with knives, making small bundles, which were combined into much larger stacks, two or three feet across, and put in baskets that Abe and others carried, balancing them on their heads back to the house. "They were heavy, especially for a young boy, maybe seventy-five pounds," Abe said. "My father said I had to carry the rice back before I could go play soccer." To separate the rice from the stalks, the family stomped and slapped the stalks on a large mat, gathering the rice in baskets. The rice harvest in November and December provided the Watson family with more than they could use. They saved some to eat the following year, some as seeds, and they sold clean rice by the cup along the road, saving the cash to buy clothes or other items.

In Africa, a lot of people carry things on their heads. "You see women with a large basket on their heads, a baby on their back, and carrying something else with their arms," Abe said. "And where is the man? He's behind her carrying a machete."

The government encouraged planting rice fields on the flat swampy lands near the coast because they were more efficient and reduced the cutting of trees. However, the Watson family lived on higher land, over twenty miles from the ocean, so they cleared farms wherever they could.

When Abe was about ten years old, around 1963, Frank built a second house down the hill, still along the main highway. Most Careysburg villagers lived deeper in the bush but living along the highway was important for farmers to sell food. That second house was a bit nicer, with a plaster exterior (over woven sticks), a galvanized steel roof, and a concrete floor. Their "bathroom" consisted of a very deep hole covered with a three-hole commode about one hundred feet from the house. It had walls, door and a roof—it was basically an outhouse. Occasionally they would pour in lime to decrease the odor.

The second house had electricity, borrowed from a neighbor, and the family soon bought a television. Abe's mother loved the TV, regularly inviting friends over to watch. "At first, we had only one channel, with some local news and cultural programs. Later we put up a very high antenna to get more stations. Then we could pick up a lot of US programs that Mom watched, like *The Muppet Show*, *Sanford and Sons*, etc. I really liked watching soccer games from Africa and Europe."

A house similar to the second house that Frank built with a plaster exterior and galvanized steel roof. Notice the woven sticks where the plaster has broken away. (Watson family photo)

Growing up, Abe got along well with his sister Robertetta. "I called her Teeta, meaning sister. She was nice, but I would tease her.

Actually, I teased pretty much everyone." Robertetta got married when Abe was about ten years old to Peter Dunn. She moved away and had five children with Peter—Jean, Michael, Edna, Arien and Emanuel. She and Peter eventually divorced, and Robertetta returned to Careysburg and went back to the name Etta Brown (from the commissioner's family where she was born and lived when she was young).

"We were a traditional Liberian family, wearing ordinary inexpensive clothes. Every couple of months, there were big dances in town that junior high and high school age kids would attend. Robertetta went to those, and later I did too. We dressed up a little for the dances. Mom and Dad never bothered to go."

No one from the Watson family ever worked for the powerful Firestone company that had entered Liberia in the 1920s. Their vast rubber-tree fields, over two hundred square miles, were located very close to Careysburg, so it must have been tempting. The company once operated twenty-seven schools for children of employees and had five hospitals and medical training facilities. Over twenty thousand people worked there. Firestone built homes for their workers, even whole towns, but the Watsons heard it was almost like a prison labor camp. Most of the employees were rubber tappers. A tapper would get up at 5:00 a.m. and tap three hundred and fifty trees, stripping the bark. Then at 10:00 p.m. or so, they would collect the sap and carry heavy buckets for miles, where it was poured into giant vats to be mixed with acid. This would form a large lump that was shipped to the US or France, where it was vulcanized and formed into final products, like tires.

The Watson family avoided Firestone because they saw that workers there lost their identities and freedoms and just became part of a machine that was exploiting the country's resources.

Rubber tree laborer with latex buckets at a Firestone farm.
(Photo Credit: Emira Woods - Institute for Policy Studies and
Alfred Brownell - Green Advocates)

"I had lots of friends," Abe said, "some older. Mostly we played soccer, sometimes just kicking a large orange around. We also made our own soccer balls. Visiting a nearby rubber tree farm, we would scrape off the dried latex along the bark cuts until we had large handfuls. At home, we pounded the latex out into a flat sheet, which we would fold around, leaving a hole on one side to blow into. This made a large sticky rubbery ball that we would wrap with dried rubber-tree bark to make a hard exterior. They were about half the size of official soccer balls. The balls could last quite a long time, even with us kicking it all over, unless it hit something pointed and burst. In later years, when the school had the equipment, I played all the sports—basketball, volleyball and I high-jumped (over five feet). Sports were how I was known. Rich Congo parents drove me to the big games."

Abe stayed in the Careysburg Public School (CPS) through eighth grade. He wanted to stay there one more year, but an incident with a teacher made that impossible. Abe was captain of the volleyball team, and the coach/teacher made him responsible for the volleyball. Abe carried it everywhere. On Fridays, teams went on the field for physical education and to play games. One team couldn't find a soccer ball, so their coach came to the social studies classroom where Abe was and tried to take the volleyball for the soccer game.

Abe refused to hand the ball over, saying, "The volleyball isn't for kicking—it's for hands only."

The teacher got angry and said, "What's wrong with you?" and tried to grab the ball.

"So, I threw it out the window. That teacher was furious and dragged me to the front school door, knocking over a drainage barrel outside." Abe admits, "I pushed him a little. He wanted to hit me! The teacher was coming at me, so I took a rock and said I'd hit him if he came too close. Saying I was in big trouble, he left to talk to the principal.

"That Friday evening, the teachers were playing the students in a soccer game. They had found the soccer ball. I was playing on the student side. The teachers were playing rough. One teacher, in particular, used his weight to knock people over. The referee was a student who was cheating for the teachers, making every call for them. A student spectator grabbed his referee's hat and ran. The student who stole the cap started a chant. 'Kick the bitches,' and others joined in, but not me. The teachers were very upset.

"The following Monday, the principal called me and some of the four or five insolent students into his office. He held a knife and said, 'You students were disrespectful. I am going to assign you punishments. And, on my dead mother, if any of you comes back at me in the night or something, I will rip you with this knife.'

"My punishment, the worst for the group, was to dig an eight-foot long by three-foot wide by eight-foot deep hole. The others just had to cut bush with machetes. This was at midterms time, and it took me two days to dig most of the hole. It was near a tree with roots that made it very hard. I missed the tests, so the teacher gave me a complete zero. He wanted to flunk me out.

"Two kind ladies, Peace Corps volunteers from the school named Patricia and Sue, who had tutored me, knew that I had been treated unfairly. They called me to their house, gave me an extra-chance test, and turned in the results to the principal. With other good work in my classes, I got an overall C.

"More importantly, my cousin, a matron at CPS (a woman whose job was to counsel students), told me about an opportunity to go to a new school for the ninth grade. The school was about 120 miles away in Lofa County in far northeast Liberia. It was called Sumo KOTA Lab School, where teachers were being trained, and it was located in Fissebu, close to Zrzor, a town of four thousand people near the Guinea border. It was a long, bumpy trip on small roads but well worth it. It was a free boarding school where I only stayed for one year, the ninth grade, but I did very well. That might have been the only year when I had a full set of books."

High School

The next year was a high school year, but Abe's parents didn't have enough money for him to buy the necessary books, clothes and other supplies, even at nominally "free" government schools within walking distance. "In our Careysburg area, very few tribal kids went on to high school. I did have one chance. A local official controlled scholarship money for local children, and I went to see him."

The official said, "Bring me a goat, and I will make sure you get the scholarship."

Abe looked at him and said, "If I had a goat, I could sell it and have enough money to go to high school. He just laughed at me. After all, I was only a country boy."

Frustrated, Abe sold firewood and mangoes on the highway to make money. "I would also go house to house to chop firewood or do other tasks to earn a little money. If I got like three dollars, I would give my mom two dollars, and maybe fifty cents would feed the family. I could keep the rest.

"Eventually, I made enough to visit and stay with a schoolmate friend, Moses Varmie, who was then living in Monrovia. Varmie was his tribal name, but he was staying with a high official, an associate justice. He had to fetch water, cook and take care of the house. I paid twenty-five cents to travel to see him, squashed in the back of a pickup truck with many others. Moses mentioned that a tough test was being given at the Education Ministry for a teacher-training high school. I immediately went out, bought two number-two yellow pencils, and went to take the test—and passed!"

As a result of this near-miracle, Abe was admitted to Kakata Rural Teacher Training Institute (KRTTI) and studied there from the tenth to the twelfth grades, graduating in 1973. Everyone lived at the school for free but had to commit to becoming a teacher. Abe had one suit coat and a school uniform, a light blue shirt with grey pants. He did odd jobs on the side to earn cash and would visit his parents during vacations and some weekends.

"There were no telephones for us. I studied hard from the start and learned science, math, social studies, civics and language arts. One semester I had seventeen separate subjects." Asked if he had a favorite teacher, he said no. Abe was afraid of getting too close to one specifically because he wanted to be self-sufficient and earn his success. They also had special classes like psychology and teaching fundamentals taught by the United Nations Educational, Scientific and Cultural Organization (UNESCO). "We did practice teaching at the demonstration grade school nearby while being observed. Overall, the Kakata school was a real breakthrough for me.

"To give you an idea about how tough it was there, I will describe the geography class. We started at the county level and learned all the key towns and officials. Then we did Liberia as a whole, African countries, all the continents and their countries. We learned the capitals, the main products, their mineral resources and the officials everywhere. For example, I knew the capitals of each state in the US and their governors. For the final exams, we were given a large sheet of paper and had to draw a map of the United States. I complained when we had to learn the names of all those officials in charge because they changed all the time. But we had to learn them."

Older students in high school were allowed to vote in national elections. This was still during the Tubman regime. Abe got into trouble when he opened his mouth in class and said, "Why vote when there is only one party? Why waste the paper?" That almost got him kicked out.

At the KRTTI school, he met a young woman named Rebecca, who was also taking teacher-training classes. They both started together in the tenth grade. The girls' dormitory was only a few hundred feet away from the boys' dorm and down some stairs. It was forbidden to go into the girls' dormitory without official permission, and the campus was too small for long walks, so they sometimes got together along the stairs to study and talk. They continued to see one another, but also others.

Abe was selected as the social activities secretary at the school, planning programs and weekend parties, mostly dances. "I think people liked me because I was a joker, although that sometimes got me into trouble. A particular girl occasionally asked if I had some change for her. One time I wrapped a snake head in a piece of napkin and said I had some coins in there. When she saw the snake head she screamed and ran down the path. I just sat down and acted like nothing had happened. They knew I was a troublemaker.

"There was a big celebration for my graduation. Everyone wore robes, just like in America. The ceremony was in a really big tent since it was the rainy season. There was music, and everyone graduating got a diploma. My parents came up from Careysburg to attend the graduation along with other friends. They were very proud of me because few people from our neighborhood made it through."

While around 90 percent of wealthy children would go to high school, poor Indigenous children generally could not afford the expense. Everyone was supposed to go to school through the twelfth grade, but most poor children left school for traditional work like farming or to help at home.

After graduation, Abe packed his bags and took a taxi back to Careysburg. He had finished high school!

Chapter 4—Work, Marriage, and Prelude to War

Teaching

After high school graduation, Abe's first real teaching job was at a nearby school in Frank Town. He taught third grade while staying in the family home, walking two miles to the school each day. His salary was seventy-five dollars per month, enough to really contribute to the family expenses.

As an adult, Abe participated in his town's activities, including dances every couple of months where music was provided by record players in halls like the city administration building. These were organized events with a dress code—all men had to wear suit coats. Abe had one such outfit he wore to church, but most didn't. So, coats were handed out the windows so that more men could get in until most at the dance wouldn't be wearing one. "It was pretty hot in there, so coats would come off anyway," he remembered. Not as many women went to the dances because their parents restricted them. Even so, about one hundred people attended each dance.

Though he was interested in government, for a long time, Abe resisted getting involved in local politics. "I hated that only one party controlled everything and seemed so corrupt. Saying that in public might have gotten me into a lot of trouble. However, I did briefly become a city council member, along with my cousin Edward, who became the city's mayor, on a careful reform agenda. We tried to give the people more say in government but had to be very subtle to avoid trouble with the national administration."

During this time, government leaders had started the country down a long path that would eventually lead to civil war. After Tubman's death in 1971, his True Whig vice president, William R. Tolbert, Jr., who came from a large, well-known Americo-Liberian family, took charge. To the outside world, it looked like a rare smooth transition of power and a sign of stability. Tolbert spoke Kpelle, using that language in his inaugural address, and tried to bring more Indigenous people into the government. This angered the Americo-Liberians, who accused Tolbert of "letting the peasants into the kitchen."[15] Meanwhile, the Liberian majority of Indigenous people thought he was moving too slowly. Abe says that Tolbert might have been the best leader of Liberia and that he did many good things.[16] He was the first to truly tax the Firestone company, but, more ominously, he opened relations with the Soviet Union, Cuba and China, trying to achieve a non-aligned label, but thereby straining US relations and support.

The act that dramatically pushed the country toward rebellion was his plan to increase the price of rice from twenty-two dollars per one-hundred-pound bag to twenty-six. Tolbert said it was so the country could become self-sufficient in rice. However, the change would greatly increase his own family's wealth, and those who were not rice farmers hated the price increase. The move might well have improved the country's economy, but louder voices said he would be willing to sell the entire country if he could pocket the proceeds. The plan led to protests in the streets of Monrovia, where about seventy people were killed. These rice riots shook the country. Tolbert tried in vain to restore order by arresting the opposition leaders, but his attempts were unsuccessful, and the disorder increased. This finally led to a military coup in April of 1980. Tolbert was killed just before boarding a plane for Zimbabwe, and several of his ministers were executed on a beach, thus marking the end of Americo-Liberian domination of the country.

Marriage

While the country was slipping toward chaos, Abe and Rebecca were doing well. After high school graduation, Rebecca returned to her parents and their hometown of Gbarnga (pronounced Banga), about sixty miles north of Careysburg. Abe says, "We still saw each other a lot. I would visit her often on weekends and vacations." Soon, Abe and Rebecca decided to do more than just visit and write letters. They built a house together, and on September 14, 1974, they were married in Gbarnga at the house they had built. There wasn't a big party, just the pastor, Rebecca's family and friends, and Abe's immediate family. Abe wore his sportcoat, and Rebecca wore a nice dress. After the ceremony, they took a taxi to Careysburg for a reception with Abe's extended family and friends at his parents' house. Over thirty people attended, which happened whenever word of a party with food and drinks spread around town. "Then we went to live in the Gbarnga house while looking for jobs together," Abe said.

Before they were married, both Rebecca and Abraham had dated other people, and each had become a parent. Abraham's son, Gabriel, was born in 1971. Gabriel's mother, Esther, and the baby stayed with Abe's parents until Abraham married.

Rebecca had given birth, also during her high school years, to a son, Andrew. Baby Andrew stayed with Rebecca's parents in Gbarnga. In traditional Liberian culture, families were responsible for taking care of babies, not necessarily the unmarried birth parents. When asked about becoming a father at such a young age, Abe simply said, "This was Africa, where such things happen." Despite the rather casual sexual encounters, an enduring sense of family and responsibility remained. Both children joined Abe and Rebecca after their wedding.

During the days around the wedding, Abe had been in contact with people from their former school in Kakata. UNESCO had decided to start an elementary laboratory school there, to be called the Kakata Demonstration School, and they were recruiting new teachers. Abe knew the principal and asked if he and Rebecca could be part of the faculty. They were soon offered jobs at the school, at $150 per month, and moved back to Kakata to work there in 1975. The school was sponsored by both UNESCO and the Ministry of Education, and row houses were built for the teachers. Abe and Rebecca soon moved to the school housing. Abe again taught third grade from 1975 to 1980, while Rebecca taught second grade.

It was an interesting school. Students were taken on field trips out in the bush along with UNESCO advisors. Abe described it this way, "Not all the kids had books or learned the materials as quickly. We went in the bush and talked about things we saw on the trip. For example, the children would see a tree, roads, hills or do an activity, and we would spell out the corresponding words. Later, back in class, the students would compose a story with the words they had learned and write them on a blackboard. It was called an integrated approach to teaching. Some shy traditional children would finally get active and involved in the class in this way. The integrated approach worked for math, science and spelling too. Sometimes we did the field trips for a week. I liked teaching that way. One of my once-lagging students is now in the FBI," he says proudly.

Abe's father, Frank, died in 1978 in his early sixties. Injuries had made it difficult for him to help with the farming for a long time. His final years were painful due to knee arthritis. He could barely walk, much less continue his work as a jailer or carpenter. Upon his death, they took him to a funeral home. His wake began at about 9:00 p.m. with prayers and words from the pastor and continued until about 6:00 a.m. with food, religious songs, coffee and liquor.

The next afternoon, after a ceremony at the church, the family and others walked behind the coffin, which was carried in the back of a pickup to the burial site in a local community graveyard.

Abe got many of his traits from his father. Frank was intelligent and very funny, often joking and teasing others. Abe inherited his father's smile and laughter, which may have saved both his and his family's lives when the war began.

Normally, Frank was very calm, but he could also be tough. One of his jobs was as a jailer, a warrant office at the Careysburg jail. There was once a dispute about his pay when he hadn't been paid for over a month. He confronted the mayor and a superintendent and said they could shove it. A woman there said he couldn't talk to the officials that way. He handed them his gun, the key to the jail cells and said, "Go to hell," and walked away.

Also, thanks to his parents, a driving force throughout Abe's life was the desire to keep learning. In 1978, when Abe was twenty-six, he started taking night classes in electricity at the Booker Washington Institute (BWI) in Kakata. With support from the Firestone company and other US organizations, BWI was founded in 1929 as the country's first vocational school. It sits on a large rural campus and today has about eighteen hundred students.

Abe finished the two-year technical program at BWI, learning many skills that were useful later, like board electronics, diagrams and soldering. Abe also learned that teaching and studying at the same time was very tiring. With his new credentials, he started to consider non-teaching options. It was 1980, and Abe's life and the fortunes of Liberia were about to change drastically.

The End of Americo-Liberian Rule—Samuel Doe

The bloody overthrow and execution of President Tolbert in 1980 was led by Samuel Doe, a member of the small Krahn tribe, who was not yet thirty years old. Once trained by US special forces, Doe formed a military government known as the People's Redemption Council (PRC). Many welcomed Doe's takeover since the majority of the Indigenous population had always been excluded from power. Abe and the rest of the Watsons hoped Doe would be good for the country and for people like them.

The PRC, for a time, tolerated a relatively free press, and US support returned as Liberia again became a Cold War ally. But Doe's broad internal support soon evaporated due to his favoritism toward his own people, the Krahn, and he was forced to put down seven coup attempts between 1981 and 1985. Doe became paranoid, worried about spiritual omens, and his government became increasingly corrupt and repressive. He banned all political opposition, shut down newspapers and jailed reporters. Meanwhile, the economy deteriorated precipitously, and popular support evaporated.

Before Doe, the different tribes got along pretty well, with minor gripes and disagreements. People would talk about another county or tribe the way someone from Ohio might complain about people from Indiana. Doe's favoritism for his Krahn area, and unfairness toward the Gio and Mano, started the country on a downward spiral toward civil war.

To restore his legitimacy, Doe staged a presidential election on October 15, 1985, which was roundly condemned as rigged. Army barracks served as polling places with his soldiers standing guard, intimidating some voters and requiring others to vote repeatedly. His government banned the candidacy of his two strongest challengers, jailed and allegedly flogged dozens of political opponents, shut down newspapers, and invoked a decree that allowed the arrest of anyone who spread "rumors, lies and disinformation." He officially changed his age from thirty-three to thirty-five, so he could meet the constitutional requirement for the election.[17] The US officially still supported Doe, suggesting that any election was better than none.

After the election, Doe initiated harsh crackdowns against certain tribes, such as the Gio and Mano in the north, and many there fled to the Ivory Coast. Doe's mistreatment of certain ethnic groups resulted in divisions and violence among Indigenous peoples, who had coexisted, except for minor skirmishes, for centuries. His survival through additional coup attempts, while constantly surrounded by spiritual advisors and good-luck charms, led him to believe he was blessed by the spirits and therefore invincible. In his ten years of rule, it is believed he embezzled about $300 million, roughly equal to the nation's GNP. Everyone knew that anyone who spoke against Doe was likely to be arrested and "disappeared."

The Voice of America

In 1979, Abe heard that the Voice of America was looking for workers, so he applied for a job, hoping his new electrical training would help. "The VOA recruiters assumed I would work a menial job at the power plant, but I got a high grade on the admissions test and was sent to the transmitter control building for more difficult work." He began working there in 1980, near Careysburg, for two hundred and fifty dollars per month. He stayed with his mother at the house his father had built near the Monrovia-Kakata highway. Rebecca continued to teach and remained in Kakata with the children. Abe visited the family every weekend.

Working at the VOA was an opportunity of importance and great pride for Abe and his family. There were about three hundred Liberians working there with about twenty Americans. The facility had fifteen tall and more than five hundred smaller antennae, a power plant, a control center and housing for the workers scattered over one thousand acres. The outer compound fence was over forty miles long.

The Voice of America started broadcasting in 1942 to combat Nazi propaganda. Ever since, the VOA has tried to present the world with a consistent message of truth, hope and inspiration. They broadcast in forty languages, today serving an estimated weekly global audience of 278 million. The VOA's promise to listeners is, "We shall speak to you about America and the world. The news may be good for us. The news may be bad. But we shall tell you the truth." The organization's reporting of the moon landing and its honesty during the Vietnam war and the Watergate crisis garnered great respect around the world.[18]

Abe continued at the VOA for almost ten years, working different shifts, always at the transmitter building. Abe and his co-workers' overriding responsibility was to make sure the transmitter was working, which involved taking the system apart each day, cleaning and checking components, reassembling and testing, all before the broadcasts began at exactly 4:00 p.m. with the famous VOA jingle, and a ping heard round the world. The third shift had to monitor the output and switch the antennas, voltage and currents to point the signal toward different regions. They didn't broadcast with the big transmitter all the time, but a smaller communication system was in use all day and night. That system was probably used for communications among US facilities, like embassies throughout Africa.

While living at the family house with his mother in Careysburg, Abe walked to the main entrance of the VOA about a mile away, where he was picked up by a bus. Sometimes he would walk the whole way, an additional two miles. He often visited his sister Robertetta and her family. Abe passed her house every day and, on his way home, would often stop to eat with her. He admits he would eat again when he got home to his mother's cooking.

The family began to grow in the 1980s. In addition to Gabriel and Andrew, Tunna Nuwoe (pronounced new-woe) was born in 1983. (She prefers being called Nuwoe.) Abe loved to play with her when he reunited with the family on weekends. She started walking when she was only eight months old. "When I got close to the house, I would whistle loud, and she would come running down the road to me."

In 1987 the family experienced both joy and heartache. Their second daughter, Nula, was born just a few weeks before Abe's mother, Victoria, died unexpectedly. "Mom died after cooking soup one night. I remember she went to bed early. The next day at work, I got a call that she was not feeling well and that I should come home. During the drive from Careysburg to a Monrovia hospital, she made a gesture, pointing to Robertetta, then me, before hooking her fingers together. She meant that we should be as one. She died before we reached the hospital.

Abe had supported his mother as much as possible. Even when he lived in other towns, he made arrangements with the Lebanese store to deliver food and supplies to his mother, and he visited as often as possible. She had an interesting way with people. If someone was unfair or failed her in some way, she would slowly repeat all the details to that person and then say, "Are you still my friend?" She would not hold a grudge. Her hard life had given Victoria wisdom and a generous heart, which she passed on to her son. Abe loved her deeply.

Abe especially remembers the quiet times with his mother, like when they went fishing together. They fished using loosely woven bamboo baskets that were attached to poles in streams. As the water flowed through the basket overnight, fish were pulled in and were unable to get out. "My mother and I used to fish that way at a creek close to our house, catching catfish, sunfish, etc. We would sleep by the creek all night talking and gathering the fish in the morning. Mother tied a basket to her waist where we put all the fish before walking home.

"I missed Mom a lot. She cared about us and everyone and never let us grow hungry. Once, I noticed that she had laid out four plates for food, and I said, 'Mom, there's only two of us.' She said, 'But there are other poor boys who might need supper.' Whenever friends walked by, she would invite them in for food and to see if they needed anything, but she always hid a little for me (her reserve).

If she heard about anyone in the city who was sick or needed help, she would visit. She took food to the elderly, bathed them, and helped change their clothes." Victoria was seventy-four when she died and was buried in the same community cemetery with Frank. Abe's sisters Robertetta and Baby Girl, and various nieces and nephews, have been buried there as well. There are no headstones, only concrete vaults made by masons.

Around 1988, Rebecca began taking classes to become a principal. She studied at Cuttington University near Gbarnga, close to her parent's farm. The children moved with her. They stayed in the house Abe and Rebecca had built just before their marriage. Rebecca completed her courses and returned to the Kakata teacher-training school, now as its new principal, in 1989.

In many ways, the 1980s were a good decade for the Watsons. Abe had solid employment with the Voice of America, and Rebecca was about to take an important job as principal at the training school in Kakata. Abe had started to build a new house in Careysburg, a much nicer place with concrete walls. Their children were growing up and living in a safe, loving home. Compared to other Liberians, Abe and Rebecca had achieved success and looked toward an exciting future. But events at the national level were about to intrude into their lives and the lives of everyone in Liberia.

It is interesting how the lives of families can move forward, mostly oblivious to the goings-on of their national government, only intersecting in a few ways, like following laws, paying taxes or voting. For many, the national drama is seen only as a show and can be largely ignored. People do what they need to survive and support their families, and the rest is just backstory—until it isn't.

Most Liberians were tired of the corruption, governmental repression and ineptitude of Samuel Doe as their leader. In 1989 Liberia sank into outright tribal and civil war. Envy, revenge, arrogance and one name would dominate the country for the next fourteen years—Charles Taylor.

Charles Taylor

Charles Taylor, born of a Gola mother, had gone to KRITTI, the same teacher-training institute where Abe and Rebecca met, although much earlier. The teachers there remembered that he was a stubborn student. He later studied to be a schoolteacher at Bentley University in Waltham, Massachusetts, from 1972 to 1977, earning a degree in economics.[19] After the 1980 coup, he served in Doe's government as head of the Government Services Agency until he was accused of embezzling $900,000 of government funds. He fled Liberia, was arrested on a Liberian warrant and jailed in Massachusetts. He somehow escaped, sawing through bars and climbing down knotted bedsheets. Some suspect that the US unhappiness with Doe's rule may have motivated the CIA to help Taylor escape and return to Liberia. In 1989, while in the Ivory Coast, Taylor assembled a group of rebels into the National Patriotic Front of Liberia (NPFL), mostly from the Gio and Mano tribes.

Charles Taylor, around 1990 as a war leader, recruiting troops on the way to Monrovia. (Licensed Getty image 51406174)

In December of 1989, a mere one hundred trained soldiers of the NPFL invaded Liberia in Nimba County. Soon thousands of Gio and Mano joined them as well as Liberians from other tribal areas. Charles Taylor recalled, "We didn't even have to act. People came to us and said, 'Give me a gun. How can I kill the man who killed my mother?'"[20]

Doe's Liberian army (AFL) counterattacked, retaliating against the whole population of the region. By March of 1990, a war was raging between Krahn on one side and Gio and Mano on the other. On both sides, thousands of civilians were massacred. Abraham and his family were trapped at the center of this bloody maelstrom.

Chapter 5—Decision Time

At least sixty thousand (some estimates are as high as two hundred thousand) died in the civil war, and about seven hundred thousand became refugees in other countries. "My friends and I first heard that rebels had entered Liberia when we were celebrating Christmas, dancing and partying," Abe recalls. "Liberian radio kept saying the rebels had been pushed back, but everyone soon knew that was a lie. Rebel progress was rapid. I wasn't exactly scared, but I was aware, and I knew that one day I might need to think fast and act quickly. As the danger grew, I kept asking myself, *Should I run, fight, hide or somehow persuade them to leave us alone?* All of the options seemed risky."

The time of decision hadn't yet arrived for Abe, though by late spring 1990, Charles Taylor and his NFPL soldiers had marched south from the Ivory Coast across two-thirds of Liberia, about one hundred miles. They would penetrate another fifty miles, to the outskirts of Monrovia, by the summer of 1990.

Families living in the town of Careysburg felt safe at first because of the US presence at the Voice of America (VOA) facilities nearby. The long outer border fence around the VOA antenna field and operations where Abe worked seemed protective of the dozens of US workers and their families. Abe continued to live in the Careysburg house where he had grown up.

When Rebecca returned to Kakata to become the principal at the demonstration school, she was pregnant with their third daughter, Vicky. Before long, the NPFL reached Kakata, and communications were cut off. Abe couldn't get to Kakata, and even the phones weren't working. Then Abe heard, to his horror, that the rebels controlled Kakata and rumors were that everyone there had been killed. He had no way to find out if it was true or whether his family was safe.

Nuwoe, who was seven in May 1990, remembers their daily life and the dangers as the civil war washed over them (with details verified or added by others). "Our family listened to the BBC on the radio about the fighting situation, and I remember my mom's frightened reaction when she heard stories about how close the rebels were to Kakata. One night I woke up to the booms from heavy artillery and the clattering of automatic rifles. We looked out the windows and saw mobs of people running, people with babies on their backs, and others with elderly parents in wheelbarrows, all going the same way past our house. It was a hot mess. We weren't sure what to do. Mom told us to turn off the lights, and we hid in the house. Later that evening, it got quiet, and a few people were heading back from where they had run to look at the damage. Older family members went outside to ask what was going on and were told, 'The rebels are here in Kakata. They've killed everyone in the city and have taken over the town.' These runners were mostly from the Mandingo quarter near the river, where the Muslims lived. One survivor heard the rebels say, 'We are looking for the AFL [Armed Forces of Liberia] soldiers and any Mandingo or Krahn people. We are also looking for greedy politicians, government officials, and their employees.'

"It was a whirlwind, and I didn't really understand what was happening. For a few weeks, I wasn't allowed to go outside the house, and no one left the yard except two older cousins who went to a community well to get water. The part of Kakata we lived in was called Dew Village because of the tall grasses there and the dew on them each morning. My mom had a bag of rice that Dad had brought to the house and a little garden in the back. We lived in the teachers' housing, which were row houses with the kitchen [the stove or pot] on the street side and gardens out back. Each morning my mom would go out and make breakfast for us all, typically eddoes, cassava, bread or just rice.

"A tall gangly guy walked by religiously every morning and my mom would have some food for him. He would say, 'Hi, Madam Principal,' because Mom had just gotten the principal's job at the Demonstration High School in Kakata, although she hadn't actually been paid yet. We would eat together, chat a little about nothing important, and then he would be on his way.

"Our house was like the neighborhood hangout spot for the teenagers. My brothers' and cousins' friends and my aunts' and uncles' friends would all come over and play checkers, cards or Ludo [a game very similar to Parcheesi].

"The fighting in Kakata had been quiet for a while, but one day a Jeep and a Toyota pickup came to a screeching halt right in front of our place. On each side of the Jeep were human skulls on sticks, painted various bright colors, with feathers and crazy things to scare everyone. I was sitting on the house step. Young soldiers jumped out with AK-47s and rushed to our house, yelling, 'Where is the principal? We know the principal lives here!' Then they started speaking in their tribal Gio language. Some of my brothers' friends were also Gio, so they started talking back to the rebels, saying, 'No principal lives here. The people who are still here are all teachers. When the war started, the principal left.' It went back and forth, and then the guy who came to breakfast every morning got out of the Jeep, came over, and said, 'This is the principal's house.' My brothers' friends kept saying, 'No, she used to be here, but she left.' I remember thinking, *We are going to die.* Those kids kept talking to the rebels, and finally, they left.

"I went into the house, shaking. Mom came into the room, saw me shivering and hugged me. She asked what was wrong. I said, 'They are going to kill us. They're going to kill all of us.'"

"What are you talking about?" she asked.

I said, "The man told them that we live here. They are going to kill us."

"What man?"

"The man who comes here every morning. He told them."

Mom went to the window, but they were gone. My brother came in and told her what had happened and said it was all true.

"A few days later, the rebels came back, barged in, grabbed my mother and my brother Gabriel, and walked them to the school. They were looking for supplies, money or food at the school and were fully ready to kill the 'greedy official principal.' While searching the school, one rebel, one of my mother's students, said she was a kind person and not a government supporter. They didn't find many valuables there and ultimately let her return to the family.

"After that, we were always on alert. Then one morning, we saw the same tall man walking down the street, and Mom waved to him to come over. She told him, 'This is not the time for you to say Madam Principal. Don't you ever call me Madam Principal.' He never stopped at our house again."

With communications down, Abe knew nothing about what his family had gone through. The American workers and their families at the VOA compound area were slowly leaving, taking the only open road south to Monrovia and then flying back to the US. Abe asked the American manager at the VOA facility if there was some way he could help his family. He described the frightening rumors about Kakata. The manager, when he was in Monrovia, was able to contact a friend in Kakata by radio, who then asked a Catholic priest to check on the family. Rebecca later said that she was frightened when an unknown man in a white robe approached her house. The priest had made a deal with a rebel driver to take the family to within the outer VOA fence, where they would be safe.

The family quickly gathered what they could. Nuwoe remembers it this way, "We all rode in the back of a dump truck with our belongings. I didn't know at the time that Mom was pregnant. My brothers, both in their late teens, had split from us and were hiding with friends somewhere in Kakata. Mom, Nula and I got on the truck with my cousin Goropu, Aunt Robertetta's daughter, who had been living with us, and headed to the VOA area. We got to a townhouse that had been abandoned by the US workers. Liberian VOA families had started moving into these townhouses because it was supposed to be safer.

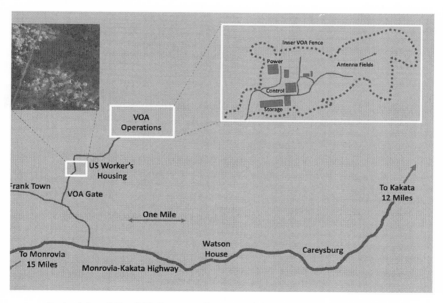

A sketch of the VOA operations and surrounding area (using Google Maps, Airbus, Maxar Technologies, 2021).

"When we got there, Robertetta was already there along with her friend Julia. We all crowded into one room. Mom and Robertetta shared a bed, and we kids all slept on the floor. Goropu slept in the closet."

There were hugs all around when Abe first saw his family inside the VOA fence. He was relieved and thankful to be close to his family again. But it wasn't particularly secure. The American families had totally left the VOA area. Only the American manager, with two Marines, returned on Saturdays by car.

"One day, the manager gathered us all together and said that if we Liberian workers didn't feel safe, it would be okay to leave," Abe remembers. "As proud Liberians, the whole team decided to keep the station broadcasting without the Americans. We workers rotated in our roles, knew all the jobs, and felt confident we could keep the transmitters working even without the Americans."

The central VOA area was now surrounded by rebel militias who were still afraid to enter the American compound, especially the innermost fence. They didn't yet know that the American workers were gone. We VOA workers started talking about escape routes, but I argued that we were surrounded and it was safer to stay where we were. We didn't want them to think we were their enemies. So, we waited.

"Then we heard through a friend that my cousin, Edward Walker, the mayor of Careysburg, had been arrested. The one who had given us this message was from a tribe that supported Charles Taylor, so I asked him to plead with the rebels to release my cousin, but soon we learned the horrible news that Edward had been killed. My cousin was another innocent victim of the crazy, insane, brutal war that surrounded us.

"As I heard more about all the terrible things happening, I started plotting how to keep my family safe. There was nowhere to go in Liberia. The war was everywhere. The rebels were even recruiting children. It doesn't help to worry or cry, but my mind was racing. Just don't say anything stupid, Abraham. Make the rebels think you are on their side, I thought to myself, over and over."

Other civilians were also entering the VOA area for safety. Some were fleeing the battles around Monrovia. They had walked fifteen miles off the roads, hoping they would reach safety.

As chaos, brutality and terror spread throughout the country, another potential leader, Prince Johnson, broke away from Charles Taylor's army. Soon three would-be presidents—Doe, Taylor and Johnson—began fighting one another in their quest for power.

"Then our American manager stopped coming at all. The Americans were gone from the entire country, except a few Marines protecting the fortified US embassy in Monrovia. By June of 1990, we started hearing bomb explosions from our locations inside the smaller inner-fence compound where the control facilities, power plant and storage buildings were located. We heard stories of children with machine guns. The rebels were destroying everything as they approached. They wore no uniforms but looted everything in their path—churches, homes, schools and hospitals, so some wore doctor whites, graduation gowns, even clerical robes. That was why Rebecca was so frightened when the priest approached in a white clerical robe. I decided that if the worst happened, that if I had to die, a bullet to the head or chest would be best since there were no longer any hospitals to deal with lesser injuries.

"We were on our own, sealed off by rebel troops on the northern side of the compound fence where we had kept the transmitter working. That inner area had no trees or other ground cover and was usually brightly lit at night. One day we saw someone climb over the inner fence and watched as he approached our building carrying an AK-47 and a pistol. He came in the control room door, clearly intoxicated and talked a bunch of crap. When we told him the US manager was gone, he hit our acting manager with a walkie-talkie. I learned later he was a rebel commander. Before storming out, he shouldered the AK-47, waved it around, and said he'd be back. The rebels now knew that the Americans were gone."

A couple of days later, dozens of rebels used explosives to blast through the fence and overran the center of the VOA facility. "I was in the townhouse, a mile south, with my family, but we could hear the explosions. I decided it was safer to surrender.

"After turning myself in, I spent one full day with NPFL soldiers, Charles Taylor's rebels, pointing guns at me. I had ridden in a dark van, slouched half-awake in the General's cold basement, been herded into separate tribes, and shoved into another van, probably to have my throat slit in the deep bush. I practiced smiling, but everyone in the hot van, myself included, was terrified.

"Much to our surprise and relief, when the van doors swung open, we found ourselves back at the VOA facilities. Luckily, killing us was not their highest priority. Looting was, and they needed us.

"They dropped us off at the station operations building and told us to start cutting wires. It was a two-story building, over two hundred feet long, with offices on the top floor, control electronics on the ground floor, and a basement where we kept supplies and personal lockers. Outside were other huge buildings. One was the power station, and another was a storage facility where all types of equipment were kept. We were just a relay station, but apparently, they thought the station was somehow broadcasting news to the world about what the rebels were doing. They even thought we were sending signals with the blinking red lights on the tops of the antennas. 'Dismantle the transmitter,' we were told, 'and turn off those red antenna lights.'

"On the lower level, they went nuts. The room was full of computer monitors, which they thought were TVs. Soon, fighting broke out over who would get which 'TVs.' The Americans had left cars, oil, food and equipment in garages and locked storage bins. Everything was being ransacked. Even though the area outside was teeming with rebels, the time for decision had arrived. We needed to get out of there."

During the period from 1990 to 1997, one-third of the total Liberian population fled to refugee camps in neighboring countries. The civil war destroyed a viable economic future for Liberia and, as the war metastasized, much of the rest of West Africa. Corruption and envy had created this monumentally stupid disaster. But corruption and envy would enable Abe and his family to escape.

Chapter 6—Escape 1

"I don't know what triggered my actions," Abe said. "The whole place was crazy, with soldiers ripping out computer screens and waving guns around. They had forgotten about forcing us to cut wires and were mostly fighting among themselves. I snuck downstairs to my locker. The lights were out, and it felt like all the oxygen had been sucked out of the place. I couldn't even light a match. At least, I thought, there was little chance the soldiers would follow me down into that black area. But I had trouble finding my locker and struggled to get it open. When it finally opened, I grabbed a half-empty hundred-pound bag of rice and stuffed my other clothes into the bag. Every few days, I had been taking a small amount of that rice back to the family, never carrying so much as to tempt someone to rob me."

Rebecca and the children were huddled in a single room, waiting for Abe to return. He had been missing almost a full day, and they feared he had been killed. Like many other families of the workers, they grabbed a few things and walked the one-mile road to the VOA facilities to learn what had happened. Armed rebels herded them together with other families near the operations building but told them nothing.

"The soldiers were still totally distracted when I came back upstairs," Abe said, "so I inched near the main door and peeked out. Somehow, I got up the nerve to just walk out the door, carrying my big bag. I spotted Rebecca and the kids about two hundred feet away in a group and signaled her to stay there. I needed to figure out how to get them to a place away from all the shooting.

"Most of the soldiers were across the road near the storage building or the power station. The situation had changed. Everyone seemed to be just looting. They were carrying away oil, gas and other things. Trying to appear casual, I walked toward the open area across from the power station near the grounds building where all the vehicles were stored. I looked for any commander who seemed rational to ask for help.

"You could easily tell the soldiers from the commanders. The soldiers all had painted faces or crazy clothes. Some even wore parts of women's dresses or wigs. Actually, they looked like clowns. The commanders had white shirts and seemed like policemen. The first commander I talked to said, 'Go away.' I tried another and asked to get a ride in a pickup, and he also said, 'No!' Surprisingly, a third commander, distracted by trying to keep order among his soldiers, agreed. He said I could take a truck and ordered a soldier to ride with us and to bring the truck back.

"I called a VOA friend, Archimore Fredericks, over and asked him to drive us. He was a foreman who had hidden overnight in one of the buildings. He also had a son he wanted to pick up. By this time, many VOA people were wandering around outside, unlocking storage caches and doing other tasks for the rebels, or trying to find ways out. We drove over to where Rebecca was nervously waiting and got my family and Archimore's son onto the back of the pickup. We couldn't talk then because Rebecca rode in the cab with the driver to her left and the armed soldier to her right.

"Unfortunately, Robertetta and her friend Julia had become frightened and left the old US housing before we swung by," Abe said. "They thought it safer to move and ended up eventually at the Firestone plantations. She and her friend walked the entire distance, about ten miles, off the road to the number seven Firestone gate. I lost contact with her while she hid there.

"We were in something like an old Dodge pickup," Abe said. "We drove to the main Monrovia-Kakata highway where the road into the VOA was located. Armed soldiers stopped us. Somebody had radioed them that a foreigner was driving the truck. They didn't like the driver or his son, who had grown up in Ghana and had an accent. Everybody had to get out and line up. But the soldier riding with us forced them to let us pass."

Checkpoints like that had been set up all over Liberia, partly to keep the NPFL "soldiers" occupied and also to prevent their enemies, the Krahn, Mandingos and anyone associated with the Doe government, from fleeing.

The Watson family experienced dozens of harrowing experiences at NPFL checkpoints, but for many Liberians, they were deadly. Some of the NPFL were adolescents, often wearing bizarre war regalia and wielding the power of instant life or death.[21] They had been organized into special groups known as Small Boy Units, who would prove not only to be intrepid fighters but also exceptionally loyal to the man they called their father or "papay," Charles Taylor. At his training camps, the children were given guns, some so big that they would drag them on the ground. Drugs were put in their food to make them brave. They were given tattoos, and ropes were hung around their necks, which, they were told, would protect them from the bullets and make them invincible. Some recruits were shot at with blanks to prove that they could not be killed.[22]

At the checkpoints, anything could happen. People were shot because of a gold ring, a pair of shoes, their accent or to settle an old score. The notorious God Bless You Gate,[23] which was named because people said it took heavenly intervention to get through it, was located in an eastern district of Monrovia. The fighters there had a monkey that they believed had the power to recognize Krahn, who were famed monkey hunters. The young rebels truly believed that the animal would touch no one but Krahn because the monkey knew its predators. Anybody the monkey touched was killed on the spot. A mountain of human skulls was later found at that NPFL checkpoint, where the majority of people who approached had been murdered.

"Our pickup was stopped two more times on the way to Kakata. The next time occurred at the number fifteen gate to the Firestone plantation areas. Again, our soldier said he was taking us to Kakata and told them to let us through. I recognized two of the guards there, underneath their blue faces and hats. They were classmates of mine from the Careysburg area and my grade school. This Firestone roadblock, like many checkpoints, just had a cable stretched across the road."

The family finally made it to Kakata but couldn't go directly to the row house where Rebecca and the kids had been living near her school. They were stopped at yet another checkpoint where a bizarre event took place.

Nuwoe remembers that stop vividly. "I was sitting in the back part of the pickup truck with my Dad, Nula and the others. In Kakata, we were stopped at a police checkpoint—just a cord across the road and an interrogation hut. Rebel police would check everything, like our luggage. We had to take off our shoes and even our socks. They were afraid people were hiding messages under their socks. They also checked for a high indentation on the men's legs, where the sock top squeezes. If it was too high, they accused men of having worn military boots in the Doe army. Basically, they looked for any reason to kill."

Abe said, "I had traveling permits, but first, the police demanded to check our luggage. Due to our hasty exit from the VOA area, the family was carrying very little, not even water. But Rebecca had thrown a needle and scissors among her things in case she needed to repair any clothing. The police said she had a weapon! But I recognized one man behind the desk that knew me. He nodded and gestured that we should not complain. He let us wrap the needle and scissors in a small bag and keep them.

"Once again, someone had called from a previous checkpoint saying that a foreigner was driving the truck. The police were starting to arrest Archimore, and someone said that he should be killed. A big argument ensued, at which point Archimore's son broke away and dashed toward the Lebanese market across the street. The boy screamed as he ran, 'The police are going to kill Daddy.' The police chased him into a Lebanese market.

"It turned out that our Ghanaian driver was more important than we realized and knew a lot of things he had never mentioned to us. His wife was staying in an apartment above that Lebanese market with the wife of Charles Taylor! Taylor's wife sent someone out immediately to rescue Archimore. I am sure he would have been shot if Taylor's wife hadn't stopped them.

"During the chase, we were left alone. We snuck out quietly and started walking back to the teachers' housing where Rebecca and the children had lived, the same place I had lived before taking the VOA job. It was a couple of miles away.

"We hid out in the row house for over two months. Of course, everything was shut down due to the war. Even the school buildings had been damaged by that time. At first, we just ate the rice in my bag. But soon, we were able to gather a little food from the garden out back. It was difficult. I had a little money with me to buy food, but Rebecca had never received her pay as principal. Kakata was a big place to hide (its population today is about thirty thousand,) but we started worrying about our safety there.

"Both Gabriel and Andrew were still gone. We learned later that both were hiding out with friends in Kakata during our entire stay."

One afternoon, Nuwoe was outside playing when she heard automatic gunfire in the distance. "I knew by then," she said, "that I needed to get low and get in the house when there were gun sounds. I ran to the living room, fell to the floor, and stayed there through the night along with everyone. We turned on the BBC and learned that Samuel Doe had been killed in Monrovia."

It was September 9, 1990, and President Doe had been captured, tortured, mutilated and finally executed by the psychopathic leader of the INPFL, Mr. Prince Y. Johnson.[24] The gunfire in Kakata was from Charles Taylor's rebel army celebrating Doe's death.

"It seemed to me," Abe said, "that it would be safer if we could somehow get to Gbarnga where Rebecca's parents, the Towons, lived, which was farther from the fighting. We had often gone there for vacations and had built our wedding house there. We were vulnerable in the Kakata house. Some people thought we had money because we were in government housing. Also, tensions were growing, and soldiers were going door-to-door to recruit new fighters. After much discussion, we decided to split up since it would be safer for my family if I weren't with them on the road."

The plan was for Abe to stay behind in hiding until tensions died down. Rebels had control of almost all the vehicles and transportation between towns, but Abe eventually found a way for the family to get a ride to Gbarnga, about sixty miles north. Rebels stole trucks, and Abe paid for the family to travel in one such vehicle, standing packed in with others the whole way. All travel between towns started at a place near the city center. They waited all day at this risky place for the truck to arrive. Around 6:00 p.m., they were told the truck couldn't take them that day and that they should return the next day. The family walked back to the house. At 6:00 a.m. the next morning, they hiked back to the travel place and waited until 11:00 a.m. when their names were finally called, and Rebecca and the children got in the truck. Abe watched it pull away and slowly walked alone back to the house.

Nuwoe remembers the next few days this way, "After the bumpy ride in the back of the truck, we stayed two days in my Mom's house in Gbarnga with my Aunt Martha. Then we chartered a taxi to go to my grandparents' house and farm. We got about halfway and had to walk the rest of the way, a long walk. It was about an hour's drive on a dirt road, maybe fifteen miles. My grandfather ran out when we arrived and started crying. He had heard about the fighting in Kakata and thought we had all been killed. There were no phones out there, only a radio. He was hugging my mom and crying a long time. We stayed there several months."

Meanwhile, Abe was stuck in Kakata for about fifteen days, hoping the tension would die down. "Some VOA friends who had already left the country knew where I was. Our houses didn't have addresses, only street names, but friends, and previous mailmen, all knew how to find people. At that point in the war, mail and other items were sent by bribing a rebel with a vehicle. One man sent me thirty dollars, and I used it to buy a passport so I could travel anywhere in Liberia and then to the Ivory Coast.

"Perhaps the most horrifying moment of the war happened while I was alone in Kakata. I saw a rebel bleeding badly under a tree not too far from our house. He had been shot and was moaning, 'Oh, Lord. Oh, Lord.' I thought of helping. But caution said I needed to get out of there so other rebels didn't think I was the one that had shot him. So I went home without helping. I stared death in the face that day, and I can never forget what I did or the image of that man dying.

"Several other ex-VOA workers had made it to Kakata by that time, and one helped me find rebels who planned to take a generator to Gbarnga. Apparently, they needed some help and said, 'Get in the back.' I jumped on their truck.

"I was upset and frightened when the truck drove off the main Gbarnga highway into a little village and then on to an even smaller bumpy road toward a farm. People were fighting Taylor's rebels everywhere, and that village, which had houses right along the road, would have been an ideal ambush site. I was sitting exposed in the back of the truck. But we made it to the farm where the generator was located. We jacked it up with winches and then drove the truck under it and lowered it down. If the generator was owned by the farmer, he didn't dare complain. Things were being stolen everywhere.

"With the large generator, we all had to squeeze together on the back of the truck. Everyone but me was carrying an automatic weapon and a Beretta. I was sitting there with all these armed guys, several with painted faces, cracking jokes. When we got to Gbarnga, where a highway split off to the west and Lofa county, I asked if I could get off the truck. I thanked them, climbed down and watched as they continued to go north.

"It turned out that Rebecca's parents' farm was still fifteen miles away with several villages along the way. I could have stayed at the house Rebecca and I had built in Gbarnga, but that city had become the main army headquarters for Charles Taylor. In fact, nearby Cuttington University, where Rebecca had studied to become a principal, served as the staging and training area for his rebel troops. I knew that my family planned to stay with the Towons. So it seemed safer to head out immediately on the Lofa road to the farm, a long walk on a dirt road. My sneakers had holes in them by the time I arrived.

"As I walked along the final path to their house, first cousins ran out shouting, 'Uncle! Uncle!,' which is what almost everyone called me. Soon my girls yelled, 'Papa! Papa!' We were happy to be together, although once again, my family all had to stay in just one room. It was a crowded place. One of Rebecca's brothers and his family were also staying at the farm, all of us in a small three-bedroom house."

Abe had hoped to find Gabriel and Andrew at the farm, but they were still missing. From the first days of the war, it was very dangerous for boys of Gabriel and Andrew's age, around twenty, because they were often dragged into the war. The whole family was worried that the boys had been recruited or killed.

"One morning, I saw a VOA guy, Moses Mathew, walking on the dusty road by the farm. He had luggage on his head, and his wife had a baby on her back. It was a miracle that I bumped into him. Running, I yelled, 'Hey Moses!' He told me that he had learned that the US wanted VOA people to go to the US but that we needed to get to the Ivory Coast first. That's what he was trying to do. But how were we supposed to manage that? We were still sixty to seventy miles from the Ivory Coast border, and the war was everywhere. I had also received news from VOA friends who had already left the country that if I could get to Danané, just across the border in the Ivory Coast, and then to the US embassy in the capital of Abidjan, I could get $750 and find a place to stay in Danané with my family.

"I remained at the farm for about two months but started planning how to get to the Ivory Coast as soon as I heard that news.

"Every road from Gbarnga to the border was rebel-controlled territory. But we needed to get out of Liberia somehow, and I decided to go alone at first. By then, I had learned how to talk to the rebel soldiers. First, I always complimented them and smiled. Second, I always had a good excuse for those who might try to drag me into their army (bad health, pregnant wife, etc.). Third, bribe them when necessary. Traveling was always risky, but I had to try.

"The road from Gbarnga to Danané was a main transport road for goods, ammunition and weapons. The Ivory Coast was a safe zone for Taylor's NPFL army since that was where he had grown his army. By this time, the NPFL had stolen all the transportation in the region. I eventually found an NPFL soldier whose job was to take goods to and from the Ivory Coast, and he agreed to give me a ride to Danané in his truck.

"Charles Taylor actually owned a hotel in Danané. He was well connected and had supplies and Russian-built weapons flowing from Upper Volta [since 1984, known as Burkina Faso] and Libya. Vehicles and material looted by the NPFL in Liberia were transported to the Ivory Coast and sold to help pay for the war effort. Taylor also had mercenaries from Guinea and Burkina Faso. It was sometimes hard to tell who was supporting who."

To reach the Ivory Coast, Abe paid the rebel driver about fifteen dollars for a ride with about twenty-five strangers standing up in a truck. They were stopped repeatedly at checkpoints or gates along the road. Each time the soldiers would demand that all the men get off the truck and would try to convince them to join the rebels. A few were forced to go off with them. Abe and the others had to explain where they were going and why. Each time it was terrifying. When he was particularly harassed, Abe asked to speak to the commander. All this happened with guns pointed at him. "At a booth, I would slip the commander about five dollars and explain that I only wanted to get to the Ivory Coast to get medical supplies for my wife at a hospital. By then, most of the hospitals in Liberia had been damaged or destroyed, so it was a plausible explanation.

"At the border, I was asked for my laissez-passer, or passport to cross over the river. Danané was still about fifteen miles from the border, so I arranged a ride with another rebel and finally made it. In Danané, I immediately began to search for the VOA people that I knew were there. The entire trip had been made on faith that I somehow could find VOA friends who had already crossed over. I kept asking, 'Do you know where the Liberian refugees are? Or do you know where the Lutheran church is?' People helped me, and I was able to find a friend, Edwin Murray, and stay with him for one day. Edwin was a guy I knew at the VOA, and I was certainly relieved to find him. I was exhausted, but he said I should hurry to the US Embassy to get the support money. Getting to Abidjan, over three hundred miles away, required an overnight bus ride, leaving in the evening and arriving in the morning.

"After explaining my situation at the embassy, proving my identity and processing papers, they gave me $750 to set up a place in Danané for my family. They had also been holding all of my retirement money during the war, so I convinced them to give me some of that as well. Altogether, I left the embassy with $1,250.

"Back in Danané, I stayed for a while with Edwin, sleeping on a mat in his place. I didn't want my family to have to stay in the United Nations refugee camp there, so I made arrangements for us to stay with him in Danané. But I still needed to get them out of Liberia.

"I soon headed back into Liberia in a rebel truck carrying a shortwave radio (to hear the news), food, clothes for my children and the $1,250. That was a lot of money to be carrying. A first-class meal would then cost about five dollars. On my way back to Gbarnga, I hid the money in a back pocket. I did keep five dollars here and there in other pockets and cuffs just in case I was searched and needed a bribe. I told the rebel truck driver I wanted to visit my cousin and jumped on board.

"Back in Liberia, I almost met with a disaster at the city gate at Sanniquellie. A commander shouted, 'Everyone get out!' We all took our luggage down, and then he screamed, 'Charge yourself!' That meant we had to open our luggage and pull our pockets out. I pulled mine out, but not the back pocket. They searched our luggage, and he said, 'Okay, go.' As I was walking away, he yelled at me, 'Hey you, stop.' I could hear my heart pounding. I felt sure he knew I had more money and worried that he might kill me. He checked my cuffs. His face looked like he was ready to torture me, and he pointed his gun right at my head, but, eventually, he let me go. I didn't have to bribe him. He just wanted to scare me. He walked back laughing to his little guard booth, having had his fun with me. I still had to walk back between some other rebel guards and prayed they wouldn't notice my unturned back pocket. When they finally released us, we climbed back on the truck and drove off. I felt sick, I was so scared. All the way, on the ride back to Gbarnga, I had a fever and headache.

"On the drive back, our truck was forced to stop outside of Gbarnga because Charles Taylor was staying there that evening. There were blockades across the road, so we all had to stay in a rebel camp that night. My worry about the money I carried was overwhelming. I couldn't sleep, and the headache kept getting worse. I started talking with some of the younger rebels, saying, 'This war is going on so long. How are you guys doing?' They mostly talked about things they had stolen or looted—that was their main interest.

They asked where I was from, but I didn't want to say too much. We walked to a place along the road where I could buy some strong liquor made from sugar cane to share. I also gave them each some dried fish, and we sang Liberian songs together before my headache went away and I could finally fall asleep.

"We stayed in the camp until the next evening before they finally released us. When the truck reached the Lofa County crossroad, I asked if I could get out and walk the rest of the way to the family farm. It was getting dark, and at the edge of the city, I reached another rebel checkpoint with a guardhouse. It was around midnight. I yelled quietly, "Hello?" No one answered. But I knew that guards sometimes hid in the woods, so I couldn't be sure. That's how they prevented people from going in and out of the city without having a surrounding fence. After waiting a while, I risked walking slowly past the gate and continued toward the farm. Every so often, a car would drive by. I knew they had to be rebels, so I hid in the bush until they passed.

"When I reached the farm in the middle of the night, everyone woke up. They could hardly believe it was me and that I came with money, food and clothes. They were amazed. Rebecca's father didn't believe I had walked from the city. He said the rebels had been killing everyone along that road. They were very happy to see me. I was even more excited to meet my new daughter, Vicky, who was born while I was gone.

"Vicky was born several weeks premature," Nuwoe remembered. "but my grandmother had studied in a midwife class that had been set up for elderly women by an NGO a couple of years earlier, so she delivered Vicky. Grandma rubbed Vicky all over with sticky red palm oil and then wrapped her in cloths that we called the Lapa to keep her incubated and warm, with only enough opening to let her breathe. My mom breastfed Vicky, and after rice was boiled, she would also take the rice water, put some in her cupped hand, and pour it into Vicky's mouth. That's how we fed her.

"My grandpa's farm had over a hundred acres. There was a cassava grove that Dad had once helped to plant and a large rice field. Grandfather told us that, before any of us arrived, the rebels had barged into his house looting and tearing things apart, and found his hunting rifle. They accused him of being an enemy and tied his elbows together behind his back, a very common kind of torture during the war, called tabay.[25] This type of torture forces the chest out, and if the rebels are unhappy with the answers, they stab the chest, causing the lungs to explode out. Grandpa prayed that they would stop, and eventually, they let him go."

"We were never far from the war and violence," Abe said. "We often saw red tracer bullets and bomb flashes and sounds of the war, even near Gbarnga. Our family had never liked the Doe government much, and we had hoped that Taylor's army would just take over quickly and form a good government." The NFPL army was winning, but Abraham had lost his job and career, his home, his sons, and now they were hiding on a wilderness farm, having lost the secure lives they had built.

Chapter 7—Escape 2

"After sleeping for a long time to recover, I told Rebecca that we needed to start packing. Feeling more confident after my solo trip, I knew we needed to get to the Ivory Coast as a family. Also, a country with actual health services would be best for the baby. Showing the money and new clothes I had brought for everyone, and talking about a possible trip to the US, made the whole family excited.

"Andrew and Gabriel were still missing," Abe said, "so I asked a rebel friend to search for them and tell them to find us in Danané in the Ivory Coast. Within days the family was packed and ready to go. Again, I arranged for a rebel van to carry us to and across the border. We learned later that the driver had stolen the van, but he was happy to get paid to take us and others."

During the ride, at every gate, Abe repeated what he called his diplomatic talk. "I would ask, 'Who is the commander here? May I talk to him please?' Then I bribed the commander with maybe five dollars. 'You are doing a very good job fighting for the cause,' I would say. 'I'm taking my wife and new baby to the Ivory Coast for treatment. I'll be back in a few days. We don't speak French, so we have to come back.' Most important was to never argue with the checkpoint guards since they were looking for any excuse to kill you. I told my family to smile a lot."

At one checkpoint, they saw Rebecca's credentials, and one guard said, "We have an educated woman here." They talked about sending her to be a trainer at Taylor's recruiting site, but nothing came of it, and they eventually let the family go on.

Most of the guards and other rebels were desperate. They had joined Taylor's army to avoid starvation, or because their lives were threatened, or so they could take revenge on someone who had cheated or wronged them. Even a teacher who had given them a bad grade was excuse enough to kill. Taylor avoided paying his rebels by encouraging them to loot or steal anything they wanted or needed—food, clothing or other valuables. Ethnic suspicions and hatreds were amplified, especially against the Mandingo (Muslims) and Krahn (Doe's tribe). Rebels forced civilians at checkpoints to speak their own tribal languages to prove they were not Krahn. Those identified as Krahn were pulled out of the line and killed.

Checkpoints provided combatants opportunities to target, extort, abuse and terrorize. Many people reported that rebels demanded their clothes, food, money, other property or certain behavior at border crossings and checkpoints as the "price" of gaining passage without harm.

"We were stopped often," Abe remembered, "at least six times along the sixty-mile road to the border." Many rebels didn't have enough to eat, so they forced travelers to give them food, especially market people. Traveling with our family was a woman with three or four large containers of expensive red palm oil. She didn't want to give the gate people any of her oil that she intended to sell in Danané, and she wouldn't stop talking."

Nuwoe has this memory about her. "The other woman, the one carrying the palm oil, was a pain in the butt. Every time we were stopped along the road, the rebels would put sticks in her palm oil containers to make sure she wasn't hiding any weapons. And every time, she would argue and scream at them. She had several five-gallon tubs of the valuable red oil that was used in almost all Liberian cooking. I thought, *Lady, do you want to argue, or do you want to live?*"

Abe asked the woman to just give the rebels a little palm oil, but she refused. "So I was forced to get out and sweet talk the rebel commander. That worked pretty well, and they let us pass until the two final gates. Near Sanniquellie, I gave my diplomatic talk one more time and said we would be back.

"The commander at the shack immediately said, 'What are you going to bring to me?'

'What do you want?'

'Can you bring me a shirt?'

'What size?' I asked.

'Size 15.'

'Okay,' I said, 'I'll be there for three days. I have to come back through this gate, but what if I don't see you?' Then he introduced me to another commander, and I thought, *He actually believes me.*

'Okay,' I said, 'if I get lucky, I'll buy a shirt for you both.'

"And they released us."

The final gate, the main gate, was near the Cavalla River at the border with the Ivory Coast. The commander in that gate shack had a reputation for killing people. They forced all of us in the van to get out to be inspected and to show our traveling papers. "As I approached the booth," Abe remembers, "the commander pulled out a gun and placed it on the table. I showed him our family papers. It took a long time before he gave us the final okay to pass. Those long waits were always terrifying.

"Our driver wasn't so lucky. The border guards were demanding money from him. We didn't know if he would ever be allowed to drive across, especially in a stolen van. So we just started walking, with all the kids, across the six-hundred-foot-long bridge. Rebecca was carrying baby Vicky. Our luggage was still in the van, and we needed it to get across somehow too."

Nuwoe remembers the bridge crossing vividly. "Walking over the wobbly and very high bridge was terrifying. I was scared to even look down. Dad told us, 'Just keep walking, keep walking.' That had been his only goal for months—to get his family out of Liberia. He wouldn't let us fail now."

Abe says, "I was thankful when we reached the opposite shore. It was like a cold glass of water on a hot day. But I couldn't celebrate yet. We still had a long way to go to reach Danané. We had no luggage and knew that Taylor's rebels were there, too, and still had influence. Then I saw the Ivory Coast guards, looking professional and confident in brightly colored uniforms, and felt relieved. They checked our papers and let us right in. Yay! We sat there for a while, waiting for the van. The children were wandering nearby, and I wasn't much worried that they were in danger. I thought, *We're in a very different country now.*

"Finally, the van came, and we all climbed on board. We didn't ride too far before the van's engine started smoking, and at a steep hill, it stopped. There was a lot of weight still in the van, like the palm oil lady's containers. She had walked over the bridge with us and asked if she could carry Vicky. Rebecca had refused, afraid that she might run off with the baby.

It turned out that someone had mixed fuel oil with the gasoline. I had no interest in figuring out what crazy person had done that. There were a lot of crazy people.

"While we were all standing around the smoking van, a woman pulled a letter out of her shoe that someone had asked her to carry across the border. Another woman who had been riding with us through a few stops, a rebel lady in normal clothes, pulled out a gun and said, 'Oh, so that's how you carry information.' She tore up the letter and said, 'We are going to start stripping you all at the gate, so that won't happen anymore. We're going to charge you all.' Then she forced the woman who had the letter to strip off all her clothes for a more thorough search. She also threatened to take the woman back to Monrovia. She dug through all of our luggage. Everyone got quiet and stared at her until she finally said we could go on.

"My family simply started walking up the steep hill carrying our luggage because there was nothing else to do. Danané was still over twenty miles away. At the top of the hill, the van reappeared. Somehow the driver had gotten it moving again, so we all climbed aboard. We rode down the hill, and then the van broke down completely.

"Luckily, I saw a man with a nine-passenger Peugeot taking riders toward the river. I flagged him down, and we talked. I showed him some money and asked if he could help us get to Danané. 'I want to charter your van, man,' I said."

He said, "I'm just driving to the river. Wait here, I'll be back."

"So, we waited, probably ninety minutes, before he finally returned with his empty Peugeot. The palm oil lady and others were still sitting in the original broken-down van, but I just didn't have time to worry about them. We jumped into the Peugeot and left them all behind. We left the terror, the civil war, Liberia and our old lives behind. Something new and uncertain stood in front of us."

Chapter 8—Life in the Ivory Coast

Arrival

"At the edge of Danané, we were stopped briefly again to show our papers, and then we caught a taxi to my friend Edwin Murray's house. We arrived around 7:00 p.m. and were greeted by millions of mayflies attracted to his house lights. We had to wave our arms around just to walk through the swarms. It was the one night annually that these mayflies came out everywhere in West Africa. Some people eat them.

"It was great to finally get there. We shook hands, friend to friend, and there were smiles all around.

"Mr. Murray had two houses—with a toilet on a pathway in between. It was crowded there with his nine children but fun for my girls, Nuwoe and Nula, because there were finally kids their own age. I went out right away and bought a few traditional Ivory Coast mattresses, sort of a long bag with a slit down the center that we stuffed with straw or soft palm leaves. The mattresses were everywhere, even on the pathway between the houses. During the day, when visitors were expected, we quickly moved all the mattresses out of the way.

"We lived there for two weeks while I walked around searching for a more permanent place to stay. My children kept telling me to hurry. They were bored in that house and with sleeping on the lumpy mattresses. I told them, 'I'm doing my best. I don't know this town.' It took some time—I had to ask around. Some VOA guys already there pointed me in a couple directions, but the owners often spoke only French or a tribal language called Yacouba [sometimes called Dan], spoken by about eight hundred thousand people in the Ivory Coast. Even some who understood English would pretend that they didn't. It was also a problem when buying food and other things. I think they just didn't like outsiders.

"There wasn't a US Embassy in Danané, but there was a rather large United Nations (UN) presence, including several refugee camps. I really didn't want my family to have to live in the UN refugee camps. Liberian refugees who were desperate for food and shelter went there, but it was dangerous. Everyone slept on the ground in tents. It was my job to protect our family.

"Finally, I came across a guy who used to be a sea hauler but couldn't find work. A friendly man, he spoke English all mixed up with French. His name was Toure, and he was Muslim. He said he could give me a house but said we couldn't use toilet tissue in the bathroom. It was their custom to use water only from a teakettle to wash one's butt and then wash your hands. At every house, by the door, you would find shoes and a teakettle. Before you went in, you were supposed to wash your nose and behind your ears. Luckily, he thought we were being paid well because we were connected to the US. He needed the money, so he agreed to let us use toilet tissue and the regular toilet and rented us the place."

To actually pay the rent of about twenty dollars per month, Abe needed to make monthly trips to the US embassy in Abidjan, the capital of the Ivory Coast, to receive a portion of his retirement fund.

The house they rented from Mr. Toure had two rooms with a pathway to an outside communal toilet, very similar to Mr. Murray's house. When they first arrived, both Andrew and Gabriel were still missing. Abe knew a man from Careysburg who was friends with a rebel who had a Volkswagen. That man became the way of communicating and sending messages and items back and forth to Liberia, both to Abe's sister Robertetta and Rebecca's parents. "We sent out a letter about exactly where we were staying and hoped our sons would get the message somehow. We really had no idea where they were.

"But Gabriel and Andrew did get the message and eventually found their way to be with us. One day, they just showed up, and the family was almost overwhelmed with joy. They told a story about how they had been stranded along the way and thought they would be caught but eventually made it through all the checkpoints. They had arrived with a Muslim friend named Swaray. I rented the second house for Andrew, Gabriel and Swaray. Swaray was a nice guy, and we were happy to help him because the rebels were killing all the Muslims in Liberia. Eventually, Gabriel and Andrew invited a couple more friends to stay with them, so five were staying at Mr. Toure's nearby second house."

"It was amazing that they were all able to survive," Nuwoe said, "especially because my brothers were the perfect age to be dragged into the rebel army or killed. It's who you know. If you have good friends, they can tell you who to trust and who to avoid. If you were mean before the war, they would find a reason to kill you. If you had been nice and had done something to help someone, they would tell others about your good deed and kindness. Our house had been the hangout spot. Everyone knew and liked my brothers. Somehow not one member of our family died in the war. Not bad— about 15 percent of the entire Liberian population was killed in that first civil war."

Gabriel tells this story about their time in hiding and eventual escape to the Ivory Coast. "The entire time, we hid out in Kakata, often with friends. One key strategy was moving about so the authorities didn't know where we were. We had friends, old classmates, who knew what the rebels were doing or were rebels themselves. They protected us. It was always dangerous. One time we were arrested and thrown in a cell. We were stuck there from 10:00 a.m. to 8:00 p.m. A dead man was also in the same cell. He had been there for some time because he had started to rot and smelled terrible. Thank goodness they let us out.

"When we got word that the family had made it to Danané, we asked a rebel friend to help with transportation. Riding in a truck, we were stopped at dozens of checkpoints, and, like Abraham, we bribed the guards at each stop. Money was the key if you could hang onto it and avoid getting robbed along the way. We were super happy to join the family again in a safe place."

Abe said, "For the first months in Danané, we went to the UN refugee camp in our area, Yankley-2, to get food for the day. Even though the food was for refugees, the local French-speaking people would push their way into the line to also get food, saying they were hungry too. Each town area had a UN distribution center in a tent with food stacked up.

"Living in the Ivory Coast was hard for us. Though I thought of everyone as an African brother, Ivory Coast people said I needed to speak French, even at a hospital we visited. I'm not sure if the language was the key problem or if they just didn't like Liberian immigrants.

"After a while, I wanted to get into some activity, so I walked to a Baptist church a couple miles away in Hooverville. The pastor there had lived in Liberia once and was responsible for distributing American aid to Liberians in Danané. When I learned that they were also thinking about opening a school in the church for Liberians, I volunteered to teach. The money for this new school came from the Seventh Day Adventist (SDA) churches, who had decided to work with the Baptist pastor. The school was to be located in the large Baptist church/house building, which would also serve food to the children. It was also the pastor's home. I was one of four people selected to be teachers, at four hundred French francs per month, about fifteen US dollars, barely enough for survival."

Soon Abe was teaching there and suggested they start a small farm on land near the church to help feed the children. "All the teachers and one assistant pastor agreed that it was a good idea, but the reverend, the head pastor, didn't want to directly give us any money for the farm idea. He wanted to control all funds at the church, including the farm, even though we all knew how to do it better than he did. We cleared about two acres with machetes and started to plant. Then I opened my big mouth and got into serious trouble.

"Money was always a somber discussion at the church. The pastor often preached that God asks everyone to give 10 percent of their earnings to the church, to which I had no objection. But one woman, her husband, and their three children helped out at the church for free. They seemed thin and undernourished. The family was only receiving food at the church, no pay. I said, at a big meeting with all the members of the church, that I was willing to give my 10 percent to support the poor family and suggested the same for all four teachers. The pastor became very angry, saying, 'You give the money to the church, I know what to do with it.'

"That idea had only been a suggestion, but soon, after only three months in the Ivory Coast, I was fired. Only the pastor's ideas were good at that church. There was no Seventh Day Adventist person at the school or church that he had to report to. The other teachers were all supportive of my idea but afraid to talk. One night I went for a walk with one of the deacons, and some others, looking for some palm wine, which was sort of a tradition among Liberians. The deacon was close to the pastor, and he told me that I was right about everything I had said. I told him, 'Let's not talk about this anymore. Let's get the wine and enjoy the evening.' I thought as long as God can support the lives of the tiny ants, he will support me. My family will survive.

"I kept going to the church service every Sunday. The pastor really didn't like that. He was angry every time he saw me. When he preached about sinners, I became the subject and predicate of his sermons. For example, he would say, 'In Heaven, there were instigators and troublemakers.' Everyone would turn around and look at me. There were a lot of Liberians there, maybe a hundred every Sunday, looking at me. This pastor was, in my opinion, extremely corrupt. But I kept attending that church for the entire year and a half we were there, partly just to bother him. But I was back to not working and having to go to Abidjan for money each month."

The children, however, felt safe and content. Nuwoe said about those times, "We were reasonably happy there. At first, I was going to the UN school and learning French. Learning a new language is easier if you are young. We also learned how to speak Yacouba, a very common language in that area. The school had a big program on United Nations Day, October 24. All the children wore matching T-shirts, and we put on a full-day program. I had a big part."

The Liberian community eventually formed a school for English speakers that wasn't tied to the Baptist church. They found a big house that wasn't completed and set up the school there, not far from where the family was staying. Nuwoe went to that school during the year and a half they lived in the Ivory Coast. Nula was still too small for school.

Abe was learning French, too, in evening classes. He says, "It was important to learn at least the nouns to be able to shop and for other things. The grammar was kind of backward English. I still remember a lot of the French words."

There were still reminders and worries about the Liberian civil war in the Ivory Coast. Abe mentioned some frightening examples. "I bumped into a person I knew from Kakata who had been friendly with the rebels and even used to play guitar for Charles Taylor. He and a couple friends came to visit me. After I cooked and we ate supper, they said, 'Walk with us for a while.' We went about two or three miles from where I lived, and they pointed out the Hotel Leon and said, 'That's where Charles Taylor used to live.' I thought to myself, *Abraham, this is not a place you want to be*. Everyone knew that people in that area had knives and guns, and if you said something bad about Charles Taylor, you could be kidnapped.

"In that area, you could be quietly eating at a restaurant, and a French-speaking person might yell, 'Se dépêcher,' or Move quick! All the Liberians had to get off the streets and to their homes quickly because a convoy of arms was coming through. Arms were smuggled all across the Ivory Coast from Burkina Faso to the war in Liberia. They didn't want spies to see what they might be bringing through. That's why we generally needed to stay away from that road.

"When we were in the Ivory Coast, we always had to be suspicious and read between the lines. It was like being back in Liberia—we had to know what to say. One day, a VOA friend of mine introduced me to a French official at his house. The guy could have been a soldier, immigration official or police since they all wore similar uniforms. After we chatted a while, the man picked up three rocks, held them out and said, 'These three are Charles Taylor, Prince Johnson and Samuel Doe. Which one do you like?' I pretended that I didn't understand French well, and I hemmed and hawed, and finally said 'Excusez-moi, répéter' (excuse me, repeat). I was sure I didn't like Charles Taylor by that time, but I felt his name would be safest. So I stared at him and eventually said, 'Charles Taylor si bon' (is good). He finally smiled and shook my hand."

That's how Abe and his family spent their year and a half in the Ivory Coast—relieved to be out of the war zone, leading partly normal lives, scraping by financially, and nervous about every new person they met. They had been told that the US was trying to get them to safety in America, but they didn't know if that was really true.

Indeed, the US embassy had been keeping track of all the former VOA workers living in the Ivory Coast. Abe recalls, "They sent doctors, immigration, all kind of people to check our health and character. They interviewed all of us separately, even the children, checking to see if our stories were the same. For example, they wanted to be sure Rebecca and I were married. The interviews were held at the main UN facility near the refugee camp, a few miles from our house.

"Shortly before we left, I was called in for a final interview. A man asked what part of the US we would like to go to. I said, 'I don't know.' They put me on a waiting list while they searched for a sponsor. Soon we learned that Lutheran Social Service (LSS) was willing to sponsor our family and that they had found Good Shepherd Lutheran Church in Moorhead, Minnesota, as our co-sponsor. I learned the good news at the UN headquarters from a listing up on a bulletin board that I checked often. On September 16, 1992, I read 'Watson family going to Moorhead, Minnesota.' Some friends with me said, 'Whoaaaaa.' I didn't know what they meant, whether they knew it was cold there or just because they were happy that we made the list. I thought, *Well, people live there, it must be okay.*

"We had only a day before we were scheduled to leave, so we quickly gathered everything we owned that was too big or awkward to carry to America and arranged with the friend of a rebel to send it all to my sister, Robertetta, back in Careysburg on a truck. It was a panicky time. For the trip to America, we only carried one suitcase each.

"I wanted to be sure I had paid all my debts before we left, including the big one—our rent. After paying that, I soon learned that we had very little money left. On an earlier trip to the US Embassy, I had withdrawn all that remained of my retirement fund. As we prepared to leave, I learned that my retirement money was almost all gone. We were nearly penniless.

"In addition to all our normal expenses, Rebecca had been sending money back to Liberia to help her parents and sister. I was unhappy with her because she hadn't told me, and even when I asked her, she wouldn't admit it. When we got on the plane for America, we only had twenty dollars left from my entire retirement fund."

Airplane Ride to America

"The day we left was very busy. We took a taxi to the UN refugee site, where they loaded us onto a bus for a trip to Abidjan. The whole family loaded the crowded bus with our luggage—Rebecca, Nuwoe, Nula, Vicky, Gabriel, Andrew and me. I was both happy and excited—my family would finally be safe in a new land. We had lived in the Ivory Coast for eighteen months, but that was coming to an end."

Nuwoe, who was nine years old at the time, remembers, "First, we had to get on a bus to go to the big city of Abidjan, a four-hour ride, with stops at towns along the way. Then we took another bus to a place where the UN and Lutheran Social Service were registering everyone. We then took another bus to the airport. Getting on the plane was kind of a big deal—a huge deal. It wasn't anything like I had imagined. People had said a plane was a large thing, and I thought there'd be space to run around and play. When I saw a bunch of rows of seats, I thought, *I can't play on this thing.*

"It was a TWA plane, and we all got little flyer wings to pin on. The flight was one of the scariest things I have ever experienced—the turbulence was awful. Oh gosh, even now, I don't like planes. Once I made us drive from Minnesota to North Carolina and then to New York and back because I refused to fly."

For Abe, the flight was a frantic blur. "I had never been on a plane before. I didn't care about the details—a warm feeling just washed over me. All my big worries were over. Other VOA guys I knew were on there too. Despite the bumpy plane ride—I kept looking out the little window at the wing bouncing up and down—I felt we were safe. But our future was a mystery, so I prayed a lot. Seeing the skyscrapers of New York City from the air was very exciting after the long flight.

"We landed in New York, but our flight to Fargo was delayed. We had to stay in a hotel room overnight near the airport, and the airline gave us some money for food and things. I ran around right away because we desperately needed diapers for Vicky. I also brought rotisserie chicken, fries, ketchup and soda back to our hotel room for the family.

"A VOA friend, Bill Walbuck, was scheduled to be on a flight to Idaho, but that flight had also been delayed. So we met up that night and decided to go out for a walk to see New York and maybe have a beer. After about a mile, we reached a huge cemetery. I looked at that and said, 'Bill, let's head back to the hotel. This is not a good sign.'

"Neither the UN or LSS had given us information about how to live in America or what it would be like. They had asked if we had any relatives in the US and where we wanted to live. They mostly just wanted to be sure we got through the airports safely until the co-host took over.

"The next morning, we got ready for our flight to Fargo. The UN representative who had accompanied us on the first flight made sure we got on the correct plane. He ran around helping all the VOA people.

"You know, people are funny. Some, like the UN representative, are ready to help anyone. But other people won't lift a finger if you have an accent. While we were in the New York airport, I saw a woman, I think from Iraq, who was asking an officer where there was water to drink. She didn't speak English much, so she was waving her arms and making drinking motions. The official was totally ignoring her. After a while, it really bothered me. I went to the officer and told him that she was asking for a place to get water. Only then did he show her where a fountain was.

"We arrived in Fargo-Moorhead on September 18, 1992. Getting off the plane and walking toward the terminal I was still worried—where are we going? Is anyone coming for us? After all I had gone through, this was one of the deepest fears of my life. It was like being born again and helpless, like a baby, having lost all resources except myself and my family, entering a mysterious new world.

"Then, as soon as we entered the terminal, there was this big banner—*Welcome Watson Family*. I looked around, and everyone was white, not a single black person at all. But a large delegation from the Good Shepherd Lutheran Church was there to greet us. They were smiling and laughing and saying 'Welcome!' They came right up and shook our hands. I finally knew that we were in a safe place. Tears of joy were in my eyes."

Chapter 9—Culture Shock: Fargo-Moorhead

Life in the Cold Country

"When we were still in the Ivory Coast, I was told about the cold in the place we were going. One friend opened his refrigerator and pointed at the frost."

Fargo-Moorhead straddles the Red River of the North, with Moorhead on the Minnesota side and Fargo on the western side in North Dakota. The cities, with a total population of about 250,000, are surrounded by deep, flat, fertile farmland where wheat, soybeans, sugar beets and corn are grown in the summer but where nothing stops icy winds from blowing across the fields in winter. The inhabitants are mostly descended from Northern European countries that have adapted to the cold.

"Pastor Bergquist, Leonard Cook, and other church people introduced themselves at the airport gate, and we stayed there for some time talking. We were told we would be staying with Mr. Cook, so we walked together to his van after getting our bags. Outside, it seemed chilly. It was maybe forty or fifty degrees Fahrenheit, which was cold to us. We drove with the Cook family, Faye, Leonard and their three children, to their home on Fifth Street in Moorhead. We moved our things to their basement family room and lived with them for three months.

"The Cook family had a nice house. It had only one kitchen, so they cooked for us, and we always ate together. We learned about pizza. I ate so much the first time that I got a little sick, but afterwards, that's all my kids wanted to eat. One day as we were eating lunch, another guest, a woman named Clarissa, said, 'Oh, look, it's snowing.' I looked out and saw white particles coming down. It was about the twenty-sixth of October, and the ground was brown. An hour later, the ground was all white. Someone in the Cook family said, 'It's nice out.' and I thought, *What are we doing here?*

"Luckily, Pastor Jim Bergquist, with his big voice, said, 'Abraham, I will feel guilty if I don't get some warm clothes for you with winter coming.' He drove us to a mall in West Fargo and got my whole family winter clothes."

Nuwoe remembers running outside in that first snow, in shorts and a tank-top, and then running back into the house to put on her new coat. "I told Papa, 'It's really cold outside.' But the snow was fun to play in, and we made our first snowman. A couple days later, we went out for trick-or-treating—America was all so crazy!

"We liked the Cook family a lot," Nuwoe said, "and we ended up renting a house only a few blocks away on Eighth Street, near Moorhead State College [now known as Minnesota State University, Moorhead]. Later, we moved to a house on Fourth Street. I was nine years old and started school at Riverside Elementary. I hated every bit of that school. Some of the kids there were nice, but some others were very mean because I still had the Liberian accent. I hadn't been in a real school for over two years, so I was behind on my studies. And then, a teacher decided to put me in an ESL class. 'Pardon me, but I speak English already! I have my entire life.' I just needed to catch up on the classwork.

"I did have a couple of friends I knew from the church, and it was a time when many Kurdish people were coming into the area. I met several Kurdish kids that I am still friends with. But there were a lot of not-so-nice people there as well. At the school, there was just me, Nula and Muhamad (a Saudi, I think) who had darker skin. Seasonally, Hispanic children joined us. Mostly I remember the very mean kids."

Leonard Cook seemed to sense that Abe needed to get out of the house, so occasionally, they would go out fishing together. He introduced Abe to fishing with a rod and reel, far different from the basket method used back in Liberia. Abe caught a large load of sunfish, far more than Mr. Cook, who said it was beginner's luck. They also prepared the fish for eating in different ways. Leonard offered to teach Abe how to fillet the fish, but Abe had his own way. He didn't want to waste the meat between the bones. Abe says, "I like the US way of fishing now, with a rod and reel. Throwing the bait out and watching the water ripple is very relaxing."

Most of the time, though, Abe and Rebecca sat at home, doing nothing, and began to feel worthless. "I wasn't used to not working, and I also worried a lot about money. The Lutheran Social Service people had helped us get onto welfare. But I didn't like to fill out the thick pack of paperwork each month to get food stamps and support money. After half a year, I started telling people that I didn't want to be on welfare anymore. Church people worried about our getting off welfare. They felt responsible for us and told us not to do that because we could lose our food stamps and other support. But I knew some people never get off, and I certainly didn't want that. I told them I didn't care about the support money anymore; I needed to move around and get some work.

"I had taught myself how to drive a little during my time with the VOA. When the word got out in late winter that I wanted a job, an older man at the church got me an old car, a green 1988 Delta Oldsmobile that the church helped pay for. He and I drove around so he could teach me the rules of the road. The Oldsmobile was a used car, worth about eight hundred dollars, with a good-looking solid bumper. I used that car for a very long time. The big bumper came in handy a couple of times when people rear-ended me." Abe claims the accidents were not his fault.

"I told a lady working with Lutheran Social Service (LSS) about my VOA electrical experience, and she found a job for me across the river in Fargo at $4.25 per hour at a company called Premier Technologies. I was part of an assembly line that made electronic harnesses—putting wires in bunches, color-coding, soldering, plugging the ends, checking, boxing and sending it to New York for final assembly in pinball machines. I called Premier Technologies the United Nations headquarters because there were people from all over—Iraq, Russia, Mexico, Africa, you name it. Many refugees ended up there. The company president and all the supervisors there were women. But it wasn't much fun. Even our bathroom breaks were short (five minutes) and could only be taken on a rigid schedule. If you were slow or talked to your neighbor, they would yell at you. They treated people like nothings.

"They didn't have enough vents in the soldering area where I worked, so I was breathing solder vapor all day. Some people who had been there ten years were still making only $4.50 per hour. That wasn't much, maybe $10,000 per year in today's dollars, barely enough to make ends meet. So I also worked part-time at a car wash.

"During this time, Rebecca was working at a nursing home and taking care of some older church members. Younger members from Good Shepherd church would help by babysitting Vicky. Together, we were making just enough money to get by."

KBW Associates

"I hated sitting in one spot all day and being mistreated. So one day, when a construction company was doing some renovation work at the church, I asked the pastor if he could talk to the owner of the construction company, Rich Kozol, to see if they might have work for me.

"Soon, I was working for KBW Associates, a non-union construction company located in Fargo. Rich Kozol was friendly, and I started making $6.50 per hour right away. At first, I was a laborer, doing whatever the supervisor needed—cleaning up, moving things, etc. The company's projects were at hotels, motels and other sites doing carpentry, hanging windows, etc.

One day, a co-worker asked me to speed things up, and I told him, 'You probably have better insurance than I do. I am going to take my time and do this safely.' He frowned at my direct reply but came to his senses quickly.

"Did I experience outright racism? Yes. One time at KBR, during construction of a new hotel restaurant, the ceiling wasn't yet up, and the walls were temporary, just plastic over a wood frame to keep the cold wind out. A guy named Gary was over twenty feet up on an extension ladder. We were doing demolition, taking down the temporary walls. I was wearing my hard hat, and a board fell and hit my head. I looked up, expecting him to say, 'Sorry, it slipped' or 'Are you all right?' But he just looked down at me. I think it was a two-by-four board, which I partly blocked with my arm. A while later, he dropped his hammer near me and yelled, 'Get me my hammer!' I didn't respond immediately, so he yelled again, 'I'm talking to you, nigger, I'm talking to you! Get me my hammer!' Some white workers were nearby mixing concrete. They heard everything.

"I walked over and grabbed the bottom of the long ladder. 'I want you to repeat what you just said,' I shouted up at him, 'or I am going to pull this ladder out.'

"One of the other guys, Bob, started to say, 'Abe, don't do it, don't do it,' while coming closer.

"I said, 'Don't cross that line, or I will pull out the ladder.' To Gary I said, 'Don't try to come down, or I will pull out the ladder. Repeat what you just said so everyone can hear.' He was trembling.

"Soon Mike, who was the foreman and sort-of my friend, saw the commotion and came by to calm me down. His sister had married a Black guy, so he knew about the African ways. He said, 'Abe, listen to me, come on. Follow me.' Soon, Mike, Gary, Bob and I all walked to the trailer office. After mumbling, Gary tried to explain he was joking. But I repeated his words, and Mike asked, 'Abe, do you want me to tell Rich Kozol what happened here?'

"I said, 'No. Sometimes we all joke. Like you might call me African guy, and I will call you back American guy. But there is a limit. If Rich fires him, he will just be another criminal on the street, drinking or stealing. Next time he says those words, I will find a sledgehammer and blast in his teeth.' No one bothered me again.

"A few weeks later, after work, a few of us were at a bar, and Gary came over to sit next to me. He said, 'Abe, I'm sorry. I underestimated you.'

"I asked him, 'How can you underestimate someone when you don't know them, their background, or anything?' Not long afterwards I heard that Gary was fired for some other reason.

"I had learned that the word nigger was a step too far. Blacks need to be careful in America, both to stay safe and to not be demeaned. People have all sorts of reasons to like or dislike others. But you have to get to know them personally, not just by their race or other things. People are people.

"During the time at the construction company, Bob became sort of my partner. After seeing how some treated me, he said, 'Abe, you are working with me now.' Early on, he got me a tool belt because he saw me carrying tools around in a wheelbarrow. We cut and nailed wood, assembled and mounted walls, but never did any electrical work. I was happy working with Bob, but after about two years, I decided it was hard to live in the United States on minimum wage. I wanted to go back to school to get electrical training at Moorhead Technical College.

"The business owner, Rich, tried to discourage me from going to the technical school. He said, 'Abraham, you will be miserable going to that school.'

"I know that when you are from Africa, some people think you will be frustrated at school. Rich wanted me to stay and immediately said he would promote me to supervisor at $10.00 per hour. He told me to go home and think about it. Rebecca thought I shouldn't go to school. But she had a chance to go to college before the war started, and I wanted my chance.

"The next morning, Rich called me into his office and asked what I had decided. I told him I wanted to go to school and continue with the company part-time."

"Are you sure," he asked.

I said, "I'm positive," and he said, "Okay."

Back to School

"As the word got around at church, one older man, Ron Jackson, said, 'I need to take you to the school.' So we got in his car. He said, 'There is segregation here, and I don't want them to refuse you.'

"He helped me register, and then we went to the Lutheran Social Service, and I signed up for a grant and loan to go to school. Soon I was officially enrolled in an electronics program while continuing to work at night putting in insulation. The classes were in the morning, and then at night, from about 4:00 to 8:00 p.m., I would go back to the construction work, nailing up wire mesh and checking the work done that day by other workers.

"But it was tough. I had to go back for more loan money to pay for books and other things. Even after I was later working full-time as an electrician apprentice, they were garnishing my wages, about $750 per month. The loan was fully repaid, but it took almost fifteen years.

"The classes were difficult too. Some were basic required classes like language arts (writing, sentence construction, speeches, etc.). The math classes (trigonometry, etc.) were particularly difficult for me, and I had to repeat classes until I passed all the requirements.

Skipping his lunch, one of my math instructors tutored me so I could pass the trigonometry test. I scored 80 percent on the final. In two-and-a-half years, I only missed one hour of classes, no days lost, never late. A drafting class instructor became my friend. I still have some of the blueprints I made in his class.

"When I finally graduated, I invited the entire company to a party. A lot of people came to the party, including my boss, Rich Kozol, who had doubted I could make it through the classes. He looked at me, shook my hand, and said, 'Abe, I don't know about you. Congratulations.'"

By 1996 the family had adjusted to life in Fargo-Moorhead. Our sons, Gabriel and Andrew, got good jobs working for KBW Construction. In fact, Gabriel is still there today. "Not long after both Gabriel and Andrew found work, they moved out of our house. They were twenty-four and twenty-seven by that time and wanted their own lives.

Thirteen-year-old Nuwoe had a key part in a school play of *To Kill a Mockingbird*. After the play, four hours long, several parents came over to me and asked, "How can your daughter be so calm, talented and patient? Our kids would get antsy and run around." Abe said he parented them the African way, teaching them respect and determination. But freezing cold and nature were about to strike the city and Watson family one more time.

While living in Fargo-Moorhead, floods were always a danger along the Red River of the North. That very flat land was prone to ice jams in the spring, and there was a historic flood in the spring of 1997.

"My former drafting instructor lived on Second Street in Moorhead, very close to the river and he needed help to protect his home. I pumped water from his basement for a while, but then went to work on the big city barrier being built nearby. I joined hundreds of sandbaggers, along a low area near Concordia College. A long chain of people was passing the bags from one to another. I got right in the line. I had never seen so many people working hard together, all kinds of people. Amazing!

"After graduating from Moorhead Technical College, I worked for one year at Red River Electric as an electrician apprentice. My boss at Red River wasn't sending me out to be trained like the other new apprentices but kept me in the shop straightening out tools and whatnot. I confronted him and, a few days later, got my last check from Red River.

"So I joined the local electricians union, but there weren't many jobs around just then. The shop leader asked me to go to Grand Forks to do some work after the flood, but I was suspicious and asked him if there would be work when I got back. He said probably not and that I would be laid off when I got back.

"Rather than go to Grand Forks, about seventy miles north of Moorhead, I went to the library and started looking for union work elsewhere. Rebecca and I had been talking about moving to the Twin Cities of Minneapolis and St. Paul. Getting away from the flatland of Fargo-Moorhead, the floods and super icy winters seemed attractive. I started looking for the telephone numbers of the union headquarters there. Finding several, I drove down to St. Paul, and after a misstep or two, I found IBEW 110 on Conway Street and talked to them. They said I could start work on Monday if I wanted to. It was easy to get union work at that time in the Twin Cities.

"We met some wonderful people in Fargo-Moorhead and others we would rather forget. Rebecca and our girls soon packed up, and we moved to begin another new life in St. Paul, Minnesota."

Chapter 10—Life in St. Paul and Minneapolis

Work Life in the Twin Cities

The family moved to St. Paul in September 1997, and Abe started working immediately. "The union had a lot of work, and there were many interesting projects over the next several years. Starting as an apprentice, making $11.50 per hour, I was assigned to Hunt Electric Corporation, working under supervision and taking classes as well. I loved that job, building a new mail center and post office in Eagan, Minnesota. After only a few months, I was assigned to a new company, which was the normal procedure. I was moved through five companies because they wanted all the new apprentices to get experience in various types of tasks that companies were doing. I worked all day until 5:00 p.m. and then took union classes until 9:00 p.m. The classes were at St. Paul College, where he first met a woman, Candace Robinson, who would later play an important role in his life. Apprenticeship lasts for four years, with incremental salary bumps along the way.

Then I took the state's journeyman's exam. I passed that test in 2001 and joined a large group of journeymen electricians who are part of the union 'pool.' All salaries are equal in the pool, and jobs are assigned from a list, where those without work start at the bottom and then move up. When jobs are plentiful, people would move quickly up the list to the next job. But in slow times, you would watch your name just inch up, only collecting unemployment. When you were close to the top of the list, you hoped they would call you in the morning and tell you about your new job. Sometimes people will turn down a job for various reasons, which they called a 'strike.' Three strikes and you were moved to the bottom of the list and had to start all over. Of course, the nice thing about union jobs is that they paid well, about fifty-five dollars per hour, before 401K, taxes, medical insurance, and other deductions."

There was a third union classification, a master electrician. Master electricians run the big projects. The test for that level was similar to the journeyman's exam but involved many calculations and economic principles. Abe never took the test for that level. It was difficult enough to learn all the new code requirements and take the journeyman's exam every two years. There was a lot to learn.

On large projects, the first thing to do is turn off all the power for safety. The key that turns off all power in an area would be put in a box with maybe six locks on the outside. Everyone had to be in agreement before the box could be opened and the power turned back on. "One time, when the job was finished, we all opened our locks, but one guy had forgotten and had driven halfway into Wisconsin. He had to drive all the way back so we could open the box and finish the job."

One of Abe's big jobs was at the Xcel Energy Center, one of the premier convention centers in the Twin Cities and the home of the Minnesota Wild hockey team. With one other older electrician, Abe installed all the ground floor lighting. He said it was amazing to watch the building going up around him. And it was nice to see all the different people in the downtown area, even the vagrants with their liquor bottles behind the transformer.

Power for the building came from a site on Chestnut Street, down below the river bluff cliff. St. Paul has dozens of tunnels cut into the hard sandstone underground for electrical and other connections. Abe and his fellow workers had to crouch as they traveled along a two-foot-wide dark tunnel to connect the power from the deep sub-basement of the Xcel Center to the Chestnut Street power source. For visibility, they connected dozens of extension cords and temporary lights, all the while laying five-inch PVC piping for the new power lines. "It was scary in there, smelly from the PVC glue, damp and cramped. We had to wrap duct tape around our ankles and pants so the rats or mice wouldn't nip at us or run up our legs. There were lots of bats too. But the job got done."

Abe is also proud of his work on the Green Line, the light-rail train line that connects St. Paul and Minneapolis with eighteen stations along the way. His main job was to install ten-foot grounding rods into the earth, which was done with a fifty-pound driving machine, held up by two men. "It was a little dangerous. Once I almost dropped the machine on a foreman when I pulled the trigger accidentally." After pounding the rod into the ground, its ohmic resistance had to be checked to see if it was low enough, and sometimes another rod would be needed before welding on a wire connector. The line was then connected to the last ground spot, perhaps a hundred feet back.

The light-rail trains are powered by elevated high-voltage lines, but the rails and towers at surface level had to be well-grounded because people could touch those. The Green Line is almost ten miles long, and it is a major transportation link between downtown Minneapolis and the State Capitol and Union Depot in St. Paul.

For Christmas and the St. Paul Winter Carnival, Abe and the union guys installed an elaborate, four-block long holiday light display at Phalen Park that cars drove through, delighting adults and children alike.

Abe also spent many years working at local refineries, first at Flint Hill Refinery on Highway 52, south of Inver Grove Heights, and later at Marathon Petroleum in St Paul Park. "One winter, we had to run a cable with fifty-eight pairs of wires. It was cold! The pairs were all colored and numbered, and I had to separate the groups according to a plan. It was so cold that I had to put plastic around the groups so the insulation wouldn't crack. I couldn't do it with gloves on, so I had to use my bare, freezing fingers. They gave me a little heater and a chair, but I had to connect all those wires to a panel, following a plan. I told one foreman that I couldn't feel my fingers anymore, and he said, 'Go inside, and when your fingers hurt again, you will be okay.' At those temperatures, you need lots of gloves, and some little warmer bags, tea-bag size. You peel off a part and put them in your gloves and boots. They help, but sometimes you have to take off the gloves to put in a small screw or something." So even today, when Abe washes the dishes, he still feels the effect of frostbite tingling in his fingers from the sufferings on those cold days.

Flint Hills Refinery, Rosemont, Minnesota.

The refinery work could be dangerous as well. Abe sometimes had to climb up the 150-foot towers to change bulbs or repair lines. They were ten-foot-wide towers with a spiral staircase leading up and around. After a long climb, there would be a small platform and a gap to the next staircase. A twenty-five-foot ladder had to be hauled up to the platform so workers could climb up to the next section of spiral steps. "We attached ourselves with belts to the rail so we couldn't fall, but we had to stretch out a long way to reach and unscrew the spotlight bulbs. It was scary!"

In spite of the conditions and the difficult work, Abe was known for his smiles. This was especially true when the economy crashed around 2008. Union guys would ask him, "Abe, you always seem pleasant, even when we are out of work. How can you do that?"

"My father used to say, 'If you only have one coin in your pocket, you won't hear any noise. But if two coins are in there, and you shake it, there could be trouble, people will hear the noise.' I avoid causing noise."

Sometimes we don't understand what workers go through to do their jobs—to provide us with necessities—like gasoline from a refinery. So many trained, diligent workers, like electricians, are needed to make modern American life possible. Considering everything, Abraham had an amazing work life, retiring as a respected electrician in 2019 in a major US city, a long way from the ten-year-old making his own soccer balls using rubber tree sap.

Family Troubles

The family's first apartment in St. Paul on California Street in 1997 wasn't the best environment for his children or anyone else. At that time, Nuwoe was fourteen, Nula was ten and Vicky was seven years old. Constant crime—drugs, thefts, vandalism, etc., brought police to the complex almost every day. One night, Abe was in the apartment stairwell watching the commotion outside when a huge Black man came up the stairs carrying a baseball bat, saying, "I'm here to kill a nigger." Worried that it might be him, Abe quickly moved against a wall to let the man pass by. The man stomped up the stairs, and Abe went straight to his apartment and locked the door. Soon there were seven police cars in the parking lot. The family got out of that place for a safer apartment and, by 2003, had saved enough to take out a mortgage and move into a house.

Abe was a strict father. He especially worried about his children's friends. "I wanted to raise them in the African way, respecting their parents and the rules." In Moorhead, Nuwoe got in trouble with Abe for talking to a boy late at night. In St. Paul, when his other daughters started coming home late, he worried about what they might be doing.

"I sat down with the girls, and we talked about how bad things could get if they hung out with the wrong people." I said, "I love you, and I don't want you to do something bad, so the social service people take you away from me. And I don't want to have to spank you the African way." They looked at me and must have wondered, *Is he for real?* But they listened, and my lessons about right and wrong sunk in.

"Nuwoe played high school basketball and would complain about people bumping into her. She wanted to whack them back, but I warned her that wouldn't be good on the basketball court." All Abe's kids loved sports. Nula played both basketball and volleyball, winning awards for being the best player on both high school teams.

The relationship between Abe and Rebecca had been strained for a long time and finally ended in divorce in 2007. "It's a long story," Abe said. "The problems were mostly financial. Our troubles began in the Ivory Coast. I didn't want to personally carry too much money, so I always handed any large amounts over to Rebecca and trusted her to handle our finances. She used up almost all of our $7,500 retirement money before we even came to America.

"In the US, her generous behavior toward her relatives continued, using much of our money to support her family back in Liberia without telling me. I was making good money, and I loved our family, so I didn't do anything for a long time. Rebecca started bringing people from Liberia to visit. She brought her brother first, without telling me, and he ended up staying in the US. Then her father, because he was losing his sight and she thought he could get cured at a US hospital. His vision never improved, and he died soon after Rebecca flew back with him to Liberia. I would have agreed to that trip, but she could have let me know before bringing him over. Later she brought her mother for a visit. Each trip was expensive. Rebecca also traveled back to Liberia to see her family and never bothered to talk to my sister Robertetta, who had lost everything in the wars."

Rebecca and Abe got counseling from Lutheran Social Service professionals, but it didn't help. In 2008, soon after the divorce, Rebecca moved out. Abe had been out of work for eighteen months, had no cash savings, and Nula needed tuition money to study at St. Cloud State. It was all too much, and in 2008 Abe lost his house to foreclosure, along with millions of other Americans.

Abe and Vicky moved to a rental place on Selby and Milton streets in St. Paul. The other children were all old enough to be on their own by then. Rebecca remarried right away but was again divorced about a year later, and the man moved back to Liberia.

Church and Community Life

"Almost the first thing I did after we moved to St. Paul was look for a church. One early Sunday morning, I walked about a mile up the main road, Rice Street, and saw a small church up a hill. Going right in the front door, I saw Pastor Carlson, a tall, lanky elderly guy with a huge smile who said, 'What can I do for you, young man?' 'I'm looking for a church,' I replied. 'Well, you found one,' he said back. After the service, three men asked if I would join them for lunch, and I did. About a month later, in 1997, I became an official member of Galilee Lutheran Church in Roseville, Minnesota."

Abe's smile and outgoing manner rapidly created lasting friendships. He also became a tremendous asset to the church, which is multicultural. Many more people of color have joined the church at his invitation. Within a few years, Galilee became the most multiracial church among the 110 congregations in the St. Paul Area Synod (SPAS) of the Evangelical Lutheran Church in America. At present, Galilee's members are over 30 percent people of color in a church that was founded by Scandinavians in 1960 in a White suburb.

Abraham Watson today (author photo).

One constant throughout Abraham's life hAbe threw himself into the work of the church, becoming a key member of the property committee and serving two terms on the congregation council as president. He started a group called Helping Hands to help elderly members with household tasks. His energy and love for the church have helped it survive through parking lot services and somehow grow closer during the Covid-19 pandemic. Calling several church members every day, especially shut-ins, became one of Abe's passions.

He also helped build a play area for neighborhood children and still climbs shaky ladders to change light bulbs on the high sanctuary ceiling. And with his low raspy voice, everyone is grateful that he never joined the choir. Recently, he was voted to represent over thirty Lutheran congregations at the 2022 churchwide assembly in Columbus, Ohio.

One constant throughout Abraham's life has been his love and skill at gardening. He gardened with his parents in Careysburg, in back of the teacher's row house in Kakata, at the farm in Gbarnga, and at the Baptist church grounds in Danané. When Galilee Church opened a large community garden in 2016, with over 260 plots across Rice Street from the church, Abe and Nuwoe immediately grabbed plots. To help clear the land, he hacked into ten-foot burdock stalks, covering himself head to toe in sticky burrs. He has been a tool repairer, mower, garden monitor and model gardener ever since. He plants collard greens, cabbage, eggplants, tomatoes, cucumbers, cassava and habanero peppers, often sharing food with Galilee members and the other immigrant gardeners.

Abe vividly remembers a night of the riots in St. Paul after the video of policeman Derek Chauvin kneeling on George Floyd's neck had been seen on all the newscasts. Abe was at a church meeting that night, and on his drive home, a church member called to warn him to be careful because there was trouble ahead. "I drove down Rice Street and turned right onto University Avenue, which was my usual way home. Unfortunately, I turned directly into the site of looting and destruction. I saw flames on both sides of the street. Police cars were everywhere, and protesters were marching across the street while others were looting and breaking glass. I was stuck with many other cars that couldn't move ahead. One crazy guy I passed was shooting a gun at the sky, and I heard more shooting behind me.

"I heard a loud boom. Police cars raced toward the sound, and I could see red tracer rounds in my rearview mirror. You couldn't drive safely through green lights because cars were racing through on red without stopping. Fire trucks were there, but couldn't do much with all the violence, so buildings were left to burn, like the SuperAmerica along Lexington Avenue where I wanted to turn to my house. Police forced me to keep driving straight on the dangerous road for miles before I could finally turn left, cross the freeway and get home. All that night, I heard sirens, fireworks-like sounds and helicopters. It was horrible.

"That video of George Floyd dying made me feel terrible too. I watched it over and over again. You shouldn't treat a dog that way. Putting a knee on a neck is the image of slavery. His legs were tied, and he's cuffed, Ron... It doesn't make sense. Even the 911 operator said something looked wrong. When I see this, I am not angry at Whites. If you like me, I like you. There is a long history before this. Not every White man was part the slave trade. People are even hating Asians now because they say the virus came from there. I saw a movie of someone stomping on the back of an old Asian man. Why is there so much hatred?

"I believe people can demonstrate, but don't destroy property or hurt others. That night reminded me of the war in Liberia. When you destroy, they will have to rebuild. Some will retaliate and learn to hate. Taxes will increase. It's just stupid. The smartphone video of Derek Chauvin kneeling on George Floyd's neck made people go crazy. Thank goodness Chauvin was convicted."

As this is written, the other three officers' actions, or inaction, during George Floyd's murder have not yet come to trial.

"When I worked at the Xcel Energy Center, one guy said, 'Hey you, Black guy,' and I said back, 'Hey you, White guy.' Another Black coworker at the center thought I was wrong to just joke back. He thought I should file charges or something. But if people say stupid stuff, I will say stupid stuff back. Some of these guys were

born in St. Paul, and they don't even know Minneapolis. I have
traveled. I know how to deal with people. I know when to joke and
when not to joke. I was a country boy in Liberia. Some guys there
pretended to know things. They thought I only knew how to play
soccer. But I love people, and I want to help them. I learned that
from my mother, who helped a lot of people. Hating other types of
people is stupid."

Chapter 11—Liberia After 1990

First Civil War, 1989–1997

It's hard to overestimate the damage done by the civil wars in Liberia, the number of years, or decades, the country's development was set back. The sheer destruction of homes, schools, hospitals and other infrastructure and institutions was possibly less damaging than the lasting ethnic, religious and regional hatreds they engendered. Eventually, people of goodwill tried to fix the damage, but a foundation of animosity and corruption is difficult to repair. The following is a short summary of what happened in Liberia after Abraham and his family left.

By April 1990, 90 percent of Liberia was under Taylor's NPFL control, including the area surrounding the VOA compound. This broad territory became known as Greater Liberia and remained primarily under NPFL rule for most of the first civil war. Taylor governed Greater Liberia from the town of Gbarnga.

During this period, the Firestone company gave Taylor millions of dollars to secure the future of the firm's plantations. But rubber production was impossible for over six years and the money merely aided Taylor's war effort.[26]

By the summer of 1990, Monrovia had become the main area of contention among warring factions. Doe, while still in office, was losing his ability to lead the country and enforce the rule of law. Nigeria, which played a major role in West Africa in general, had established the Economic Community of West African States (ECOWAS) to maintain regional order, along with the Economic Community of West African States Monitoring Group (ECOMOG) as a military peacekeeping force. Nigeria rightly worried that Taylor would export his rebellion to other countries, including Nigeria itself, so in August 1990, it sent about seven thousand well-trained troops to establish peace in Liberia.

As mentioned, Samuel Doe attempted to visit the newly established ECOMOG base at the Monrovia airport but did it too soon. Believing he was invincible and protected by charms and spirits, he drove to the airport and allowed his guards to be disarmed. He was quickly captured, tortured and killed by Prince Johnson and his INPFL forces. Both Prince Johnson and Charles Taylor continued their siege of Monrovia, but now Nigeria was playing the defender role.

A period of immense confusion began with new armies forming and splitting, new governments being created and dying, and with invasions into western Liberia, taking territory from Taylor. In September 1993, the United Nations established an observer presence to monitor peace agreements, but by October 1994, they pulled out in frustration because combatants would not honor their own promises. This confusion continued until September 1996, when a ceasefire was held with three parties, including Charles Taylor, sharing control.

The first Liberian civil war was both violent and tragic. Most regard it as one of Africa's bloodiest civil wars. By 1996, people in Monrovia itself were seeing first-hand the grisly practices they had only heard about, such as the hearts of victims being ripped out while they were still alive, being handed to a wife to cook, then shared later by the victorious soldiers. These accounts are often discounted, but they were repeatedly photographed and documented.[27] Taylor's anything-goes war had destroyed the humanity of a generation.

Soon, unfortunately, he would gain even more power.

Second Civil War, 1997–2003

With the cease-fire holding, a national election was called. In July 1997, Charles Taylor won the presidency with 75 percent of the vote, and he gained a majority of the representative seats in the Liberian legislature. The election was judged free and fair by some observers, but he did control the majority of Liberia's territory, which undoubtedly intimidated voters. Taylor had finally achieved his goal.

Unfortunately, bloodshed in Liberia did not end. Violence kept flaring up, starting what became known as the second Liberian civil war. During his entire reign, Taylor had to fight insurgencies against his government while he continued to support a rebel force in Sierra Leone who were trading weapons for diamonds. In 2000 a new force called the Liberians United for Reconciliation and Democracy (LURD) invaded from Guinea in Lofa County. Liberia was now engaged in a complex three-way conflict with Sierra Leone and the Republic of Guinea.

Meanwhile, in March 2001, the United Nations Security Council concluded that Liberia and Charles Taylor played roles in the civil war in Sierra Leone and banned his arms and diamond trading. By supporting brutal Sierra Leonean rebels, Taylor also drew the enmity of the British and Americans. Losing ground to two armies at his doorstep in Monrovia, being accused of "crimes against humanity," and with the US demanding that he leave Liberia, Taylor finally fled to Nigeria. Various politicians temporarily replaced him, but in the end, as will be explained, an unexpected new group took over.

Dozens of rumors and denials have circulated about Taylor's relationship with the US, the CIA and the Defense Intelligence Agency (DIA). Taylor claimed for many years that his escape from prison in Plymouth, Massachusetts, using bedsheets, and his subsequent invasion of Liberia, were supported by the US. His claims were denied repeatedly by the CIA and others up to his 2009 trial for war crimes at the Hague, where he again said the support was true.

His very first attempts at recruiting an army in Africa began in Libya, with about one hundred men. Libya and Burkina Faso supplied him with Russian arms. Some have claimed that he had a secret CIA role to provide intelligence about the activities of Muammar Gaddafi. Oddly, he was ultimately convicted not for his crimes in Liberia but for his role in the diamond trade and for supporting rebels in Sierra Leone. In 2009 he was sentenced to fifty years in prison for eleven counts of crimes against humanity, including rape, murder, sexual slavery, and other inhumane acts, violations of the Geneva conventions, and conscripting children to fight as soldiers. His son was also convicted of crimes of torture and sentenced to ninety-seven years in prison.

The damage caused by Liberia's two civil wars, mostly at the direction of Charles Taylor, was immense. One example is instructive. Rice production, the once abundant food staple of the country, fell by 76 percent between 1987 and 2005. Chronic malnutrition, even in 2012, had become endemic, caused by a lack of infrastructure, poverty and low availability of fertilizers or pesticides (below 1 percent). The damage to education, health systems and many other areas was equally disastrous.

The Women Take Charge, 2004 to Present

By 2002, the women in Liberia were tired of seeing their country torn apart and their families killed. Social worker Leymah Gbowee decided to bring women from her Lutheran church together to protest the war. They started gathering and praying in a Monrovia fish market to protest the violence. With media attention, their protest grew until over twenty-five hundred gathered at the fish market each day. She formed an organization called the Women of Liberia Mass Action for Peace which issued this statement to Taylor: "In the past, we were silent, but after being killed, raped, dehumanized, infected with diseases, and watching our children and families destroyed, war has taught us that the future lies in saying NO to violence and YES to peace!"[28]

Both Christian and Muslim women sat, danced and sang for peace. The fish market location was visible from President Taylor's residence, and his motorcade passed by the women's protest every day. The women, all wearing white, also agreed that they would go on a sex strike, denying their partners intimacy until the war ended.

In the summer of 2003, the women forced Taylor and the Government of Liberia, Liberians United for Reconciliation and Democracy (LURD, a Guinea-based force) and the Movement for Democracy in Liberia (MODEL, Ivory Coast-based) to attend a peace conference in Accra, Ghana. They raised money to send a group of women who gathered in front of the conference building, singing and holding signs. When Taylor learned that he had been indicted for war crimes by an international court in Sierra Leone, he fled back to Liberia, but the peace conference in Accra continued with his representatives. Calling in reinforcements, the women surrounded the building, blocked all doors and windows, and refused to let the delegates leave until a statement was agreed upon and signed. When police came to arrest the women, Gbowee threatened to remove her clothing, an act that would shame the men. Her threat prevented security from arresting them.

To end the standoff, John Kufour, the Ghanaian president and chief mediator of the peace talks, met with the women and heard their pleas for peace. Three weeks later, on August 11, Taylor resigned the presidency, and the peace agreement was announced. Taylor went into exile to Nigeria, UN Peacekeeping forces were ordered to enter Monrovia, and a transitional government was put in place. The women held a victory march and hundreds of children followed the women through the streets shouting, "We want peace, no more war!"

Over the next two years, the Women of Liberia Mass Action for Peace group aided the government in bringing about democratic elections. They registered voters and set up polling stations. On November 23, 2005, they brought to power Liberia's and Africa's first female head of state, Ellen Johnson Sirleaf.

Ellen Johnson Sirleaf (Wikipedia image)

Johnson Sirleaf, who is of mixed America-Liberian and Indigenous descent, served as president of Liberia from 2006 to 2018. The Harvard-trained World Bank economist had many notable successes.

On July 26, 2007, as one of her first acts, President Sirleaf issued an executive order making education free and compulsory for all elementary school-aged children. Then in three years, with help from the US, she eliminated the national debt of $4.9 billion. A Truth and Reconciliation (TRC) Commission was created with the mandate to promote national peace. During her entire time as president, there was no significant resumption of war in Liberia. In 2011 she was reelected and, together with Liberian Leymah Gbowee and Yemeni Tawakkol Karman, won the Nobel Peace Prize for their "non-violent struggle for the safety of women and for women's rights to full participation in peace-building work." She led Liberia through a deadly Ebola epidemic between 2013 and 2015.

During her inauguration, Sirleaf had promised that she would impose a "zero-tolerance" policy on corruption within the government. At one point, she even dismissed her brother for corruption. Despite this, critics have argued that corruption remained rampant within Sirleaf's administration and the country in general, and she doesn't disagree. Sirleaf was term-limited and left the presidency in 2018 at the age of eighty.

Despite Sirleaf's goal in 2007 to require and provide free elementary schools, education remains Liberia's most urgent need. After two brutally destructive civil wars, compounded by school closures due to the Ebola outbreak, the education system remains fragile. Liberia is still rebuilding its educational system in terms of student access, the quality of teaching, and classroom infrastructure.

Progress has been made. In 2015, close to 1.4 million children were registered in pre-primary, primary and high school. Yet Liberia is significantly behind most other African countries in nearly all educational statistics. For example, only 54 percent of children complete primary education. In Liberian schools, 36 percent of primary teachers and 29 percent of secondary instructors are unqualified.[29]

Perhaps the greatest success factors in Abraham's life were his zeal and miraculous access to education. He was able to achieve his dreams of completing high school, becoming a teacher and learning about electrical systems, thereby proving his high value in a country where Indigenous people were looked down on. Somehow, Liberia must make education opportunities and incentives available to far more children.

Chapter 12—The View from America

Abraham and Anshawn's Visit to Liberia

Abraham and his son-in-law Anshawn (Nuwoe's husband, whom he calls George) visited Liberia in 2011 to see the country and visit with relatives who remain there.

Abe could immediately see that some things were the same. "When George and I first entered Liberia, a guy sitting at a desk looking at my papers said that I wasn't ready to enter the country. I took out a five-dollar bill, and he said, 'Now you're talking,' and let me pass. George, in a separate line, gave the agent there twenty dollars. That guard said, 'Have a wonderful time in Liberia. You will be going far in life! Come back often.' Some other people foolishly tried arguing with the gateman, so the lines were very slow and long."

Anshawn grew up in a traditional but fairly well-to-do-family living in Paynesville, a suburb of Monrovia. "We weren't rich, but we weren't poor either. My dad traveled all over, studied in Germany and worked as an engineer for a radio station." Anshawn left Liberia in 1987 at age sixteen, before the war, to study in America.

Anshawn remembers Liberia as a happy place where he played with his cousins in a beautiful backyard. "My father had amazing gardens, almost like the White House, with flowers and fruits and mowed grass." His father had moved to the US around 1983.

Paynesville was the first place Abraham and Anshawn visited. "In my wildest dreams," Anshawn said, "I never expected to see what Liberia had become after the wars. I thought Liberia was still going to be a flourishing country. I could hardly recognize my old house. It was broken down, overgrown, in deplorable condition.

"I loved seeing my mother, though, and my other relatives. I hugged them all, and we took photos. In the evening, we went to a place called The Tree and reminisced, watched the people go by and had a good time. We ate well, and everything was fresh."

Abe and Anshawn then traveled to Careysburg. "We had a car and a driver for our visit, but even still, we got lost," Abe said. "After Paynesville, all the roads looked different. Even the main Monrovia-to-Kakata highway was party overgrown and full of potholes. Some were like swimming pools, not just potholes."

They reached Careysburg and saw the house that Abe had started building before the war started. It would have been a much more modern place than his father's house, with concrete block walls, but it was still unfinished.

Abe stayed with cousins and some old friends around Careysburg and made a pilgrimage to visit his family member's graves, including his sister Robertetta's, who is buried near their father and mother.

"Sadly, Robertetta died in November 2008. She had tried to get to the US much earlier and even had her passport ready, but then 9/11 happened, and all transfers to the US from Liberia and many other countries were cut off. We received a tape of her funeral, which the family watched together, crying."

Abe visited Robertetta's children, his nieces, during the 2011 trip. Edna Dunn and Patience Dlana have stayed in contact over the years. They ate together and played a lot of Ludo. A nephew, their brother Edwin Dunn, now lives in Virginia.

"There are a lot more houses now in Liberia than before the war, and many are wood frame, like those in America." Abe said, "If

I went back now, I could easily afford to build a grand new house. But I am comfortable and safe in the US.

"People ask me if I will go back to help Liberia develop. I will visit again, for sure, and would like to help the people there somehow. But it makes me nervous. What if the violence starts again? And Liberia is such a corrupt country. It's rich in resources and people, but there is still so much bribery and lying. The person who is chief of a certain county needs his payoff. It holds the country down. Our relatives are always pleading for money from those of us who made it to the US. But the money is rarely used as promised."

Anshawn, for example, wanted to build a hospital or clinic in Liberia, and during the trip, he visited two acres of land he had purchased near the airport. But the other money he sent for that project had disappeared. "You have to be physically in the country to pull off a thing like that," he concluded.

They visited one church-related grade school that reminded Abe of the schools where he taught. Anshawn visited a different school connected to Team Challenge Liberia, where former drug addicts, still recovering after the wars, were being helped. He talked to some of the students about their experiences. They said they were just happy to be in a safe place with three good meals each day. Living out on the street was exhausting and dangerous. And they told Anshawn about the dreams they had about one day having a productive job, an education and maybe even a family.

Before leaving, they enjoyed time at the beach in Monrovia. Anshawn said, "We had a wonderful time there. We drank beer. It felt like the fun days of my childhood, back in 1987 before I left. I felt at home. If you have money, you can be comfortable in Liberia. But too many people depend on the government, waiting for a handout. They are not striving for success. Too many are doing nothing.

"The big winners now are the Lebanese, the shopkeepers during the war, who have expanded into many areas. They are competing with the Chinese in new developments. The Chinese are investing in natural resources and basically stripping the country, especially iron mines. The Chinese have also built a new university.

"For Liberia to succeed," Anshawn said, "it needs a new mindset. It's sliding backwards. Ghana and Sierra Leone are becoming industrial powerhouses. Liberia needs to be awakened before it becomes the ass of Africa. Once upon a time, Liberia was considered 'Little America,' ahead of all the other African countries. Now it's behind them all, in education and so many things. It's sad."

In many ways, Abe was forced out of his home country back in 1990. "I had a good job then at the VOA, making three hundred dollars every two weeks, and I was building the new, nicer house. Back then, my entire $300 paycheck went to us—no big deductions like in the US. Over there, if you had a solid job, you were considered very lucky. I'm sorry we didn't have a chance to visit what remains of the VOA area during our trip. Sadly, the entire Liberian VOA system was destroyed during the civil war. The relay function has moved to other countries.

"We were, of course, happy and relieved to escape the war safely," he quickly adds.

Liberia's current president, George Weah, was elected more for his celebrity status as a World Cup soccer player than for his government leadership ability. He was the 1995 FIFA World Player of the Year, a distinction of great pride for Liberia. He has championed youth programs as president but has many critics for his inaction in other areas.

For example, armed robberies, public-sector corruption, poverty and hunger are on the rise. Even worse, President Weah and the country are now struggling with the coronavirus, like the rest of the world. As of this writing, only about 6 percent of the population has been vaccinated. With Johnson and Johnson vaccine from the US, they hope to get to 10 percent. By November 2021, only 300 deaths had been attributed to Covid-19, but like the rest of Africa, and with new strains of the virus emerging, the situation is dangerous.

Other Liberians in America

There are now over 250,000 former Liberians and their families living in the US. They represent large percentages (over 30 percent) of the population in the Twin Cities suburbs of Brooklyn Park and Brooklyn Center two towns where large numbers of Liberians settled after the wars, the largest number of any state (about 35,000).[30] Abraham has attended meetings of Liberians in those cities but hates it when many are still arguing whether or not Charles Taylor was good for Liberia.

He has also been invited to large Baptist churches there but has turned down the invitations because he doesn't like the long church services that stretch into the afternoon. "I like my church, Galilee, because I love the people there, and I don't even have to even think about being a Black. It is a true Christian community."

Since 1991, when President George H. W. Bush granted Liberians in the US temporary status as the civil war broke out in their home country, the laws allowing Liberian immigrants to stay in the US have been precarious at best. President Trump even threatened to end the temporary status in 2018. But a clause called the "Liberian Refugee Immigration Fairness Act," buried in the huge defense authorization bill in 2019, easily passed Congress and was signed into law.

The Brooklyn Park Community Center was the site of a tremendous celebration in January 2020 when many Liberians in Minnesota learned they would receive green cards and were finally on their way to becoming citizens. The entire political establishment of Minnesota was there, beaming—US senators, congressmen, mayors, the attorney general, the governor—they were all there for the celebration. Hundreds of Liberians shouted "Hallelujah!" and "Praise God!"[31]

A little more than a year later, in April 2021, at a location only fourteen miles from the George Floyd killing, a Brooklyn Center police officer, who said she thought she was using her taser, shot and killed another Black, Daunte Wright, during a traffic stop. Deaths like this one occur far too often in Minnesota and the rest of the country. People continue to wonder how many of these deaths are accidental, a result of circumstance, are avoidable, or are a result of racism and hatred. It is often hard to distinguish. New rules and tactics will not be enough. The answer lies in people's hearts.

Perhaps there are clues in Abraham Watson's life. He lives with honesty, ambition, hard work, humor, toughness and a smile. On the surface, that's all it takes. What is hidden in our minds about trusting "others" will take longer to heal. Sometimes it takes actually working side-by-side, not just going by what you see on TV, crime shows and news stories, or what your bar mate or relatives say about the 'others.' Working together with honesty, kindness and respect takes some time, but it works.

Abe's View of Liberia and America and Their Futures

"In my view," Abe says, "Liberia's core problem is still corruption. They have the right laws, but they are not enforced. The country needs 'honest checker people,' whistleblowers who can't be corrupted. They need to come down hard against bribery or corruption. If you are stranded on the road in Liberia, it does no good to just call the government—your bribe has to be ready. Many get jobs from relatives or big wigs. If they get caught cheating, they just go to a higher level, like the Minister of Roads, or their brother-in-law, to be let off. A lot of it is cultural. How do you change cultural traditions that are centuries old?

"Unfortunately, it takes a long time to change a culture. In Minnesota, people generally trust one another. They take offense if someone asks for a bribe. This may not be true throughout the US, but here it is the norm. Leadership is crucial. President Sirleaf tried by establishing the Truth and Reconciliation (TRC) Commission, but after fifteen years as president, not much changed."

Abe heard about a couple who wanted to start a Liberian factory and hire a lot of people. They were told they had to put down five million dollars as a bond—corruption again. So what happened—they built the factory in Sierra Leone. No one wants to invest in such an environment. As a result, people don't have productive jobs. Getting a government job in Monrovia is still seen as the only way to succeed.

"Education is the other main problem," Abe says. "The system used to be pretty good, although it was hard for poor people like me. I worked and studied very hard, but I was also very lucky. There were many programs to train teachers before the war. Most of that broke down during almost fifteen years of conflict. Many young lives were warped and destroyed by learning the war lifestyle. Even today, the former warriors suffer from drug addiction.

Young children and their families are again just trying to survive, and that means the kids are back helping on the farms, not going to school. As mentioned, only 44 percent of grade school kids are in school. The Minister of Education needs to get out to improve the lives of the Indigenous people, but he just sits in Monrovia.

"Liberia can improve. They can make it, but it requires strong leadership. Tolbert had the right idea. He dragged one corrupt minister to a flagpole and had him flogged. It was all over the news. That got everyone's attention, and things started changing; corrupt people were scared. But over the years, his successes were forgotten. Liberia is a rich country in many ways, with plentiful natural resources and access to the sea. But corruption stands in the way everywhere in the country.

"I still love Liberia. At my age, I can't consider going back permanently. On my trip back in 2011, I found it so sad that things haven't improved in either the education or in the health systems. An American friend living in Liberia told me about a hospital that didn't even have oxygen tanks. So they traveled to several others before finding one that could treat her sick husband. In Monrovia, there is city water, but only if you can afford it. Most buy bottled water for drinking. It is just sad.

"Before the war, the sixteen tribes got along fairly well, but the Americo-Liberians were different. I hated the way my mother was treated, being promised an education but treated as a slave. Many Americo-Liberians were unfair, and that still bothers me today. How my mother was treated was evil. But even in that case, people just went about their business, living their lives, no matter how unfair.

"In America, you have people from all over the world with different ideas. Yet it is here where I learned the word segregation. People openly say bad things about those who are different. That didn't happen often in Liberia before the war. We didn't make up new names, ethnic slurs like nigger or spick, to put people down. We didn't do things to hurt other people's feelings. The worst I heard was people calling me 'country boy' in school. I would just think, *You may have more money, but I have more brains*.

"Here, in the US, I keep hearing stories about slavery. I think, *Does your father know what happened? Does even your grandfather know about this slavery thing?* So if it's one America, everyone living as one in America, why segregate? Why look at people differently? Why can't we be together? Why?

"You can look at it both ways. Some Black people say it's the White man that enslaved us. Whenever something bad happens, they think, *Whites are doing it again*. They don't try to know the people involved and get to the truth. This applies to both sides. If you tell Black and White children not to play together, they will grow up with this attitude. When people work together or play together, they learn about the whole person, not just the shade of their skin. They discover, 'Hey, they're okay.'

"I don't look at color. If you like me, I like you. If you can't like me, I keep my distance. You need to know someone before you judge them. But, when someone calls all African countries 'shithole countries,' you understand how that person thinks. Some of the problem is simple ignorance. Occasionally, when I've met someone for the first time, I've been asked, 'Do you have houses there? Or do you have cars?' Do they think that we are still riding horses or donkeys?

"There are some Black Americans that don't like the Blacks from Africa because we are too polite. In the US, all are free to complain. We can cuss the president without being arrested. We have freedoms here, but some forget that their rights end when they come up to another person. The US has more people in jail than any other country, many for little things or acts of desperation. Why can't we help them more? It's not just giving them food stamps or money. We need to get them an education and a meaningful job.

"My advice: try to love one another. Get to know individuals and respect and love one another. Faith is part of it for me. Children have about twelve years to learn in school how to be valuable to others. Parents have the responsibility to get them ready to contribute. They have to have a personal foundation for life. When you point your index finger at someone like you were shooting, the thumb is pointing to God, and three fingers are pointing back at you.

"What I miss most about Liberia are the social aspects. Many people visit each other often, work the farms together, help out when times are tough, eat together, live nearby, and really know each other. Take the example of Christmas. In the US, it's all family, family, family. In Liberia, holidays are a time when the whole community celebrates together. We were happy and satisfied with our lives despite our lack of money and material things. I long for that part of Liberia."

A Typical American Family

Abraham and his family have now been in the US for almost twenty-five years. In most ways, they are now a prototypical American family. All of Abe's children passed the test and became naturalized citizens starting in 2003. Abe was a bit later, in 2006, because he claimed he was too busy with work. Among the daughters, only Nuwoe has deep memories of Liberia. Nula and Vicky essentially grew up in the US and show little nostalgia for the place they were born. They always get together for holidays and big events to eat African food. Abe admits that he has eaten monkey jerky, cobra meat and cow skin in the last few years. But in all the ways that count, it's like the Watson family has been in America for hundreds of years.

Maybe they will get a chance to look back. Nuwoe is planning a grand family trip to Liberia, so they can all experience their roots. Abe would like to go so he could begin to develop a one-acre lot along the Monrovia-Kakata highway that his father saved and sacrificed to purchase but has never been used. He is considering building a special education school or maybe a medical clinic.

All three daughters found jobs soon after completing their education and are now leading productive lives. Health care and education are a family theme. Here is a snapshot of the Watson clan:

Nuwoe worked after high school at a nursing home but then went back to school. She graduated from Century College, a two-year community and technical school, and is now a medical assistant specializing in surgical instruments. She married Anshawn Davis and had two children, Nijah and Adrian. Nijah is currently studying at Creighton University, preparing for a medical career, and Adrian just entered high school. Nuwoe organized an excellent high school graduation party for Nijah with one hundred guests. In many ways, Nuwoe is now the family glue, the one everyone goes to for support.

Anshawn and Nuwoe divorced, but both still play important roles in their children's lives. Anshawn remains one of Ron's close friends, working on projects together and with Ron tutoring on Anshawn's seemingly endless string of advanced medical courses. He currently is at the Hennepin County Medical Center as a Mental Health Worker but keeps searching for better-paying jobs.

After working for a while, Nula went to St. Cloud State University for one year until the family's money was exhausted. She then joined the army and completed two tours of duty, one in Kuwait and the second in Syria, doing mostly administrative work, never carrying a gun into battle. An introvert, Nula doesn't often speak about her time in the army. She's now working at Health East, taking classes and continuing to serve as a sergeant in the National Guard.

One time, between her deployments, Nula came back to Minnesota without telling Abe. He got a call from Nuwoe saying that he needed to hurry over because she was sick and needed a ride to the hospital. "I went running, speeding over there, and as the door opened—Ta da! There was Nula. My feelings were happily jolted. Nuwoe was okay, and there was Nula!"

The youngest daughter, Vicky, took courses in cosmetology, but the school closed down before she finished. She, too, is working, but like many in her generation, she is an independent soul, managing her life without asking for help, sort of a "village" person—a total American. If Abe asks too much about what she is doing, she gets upset. Details of her life are a bit of a mystery.

Gabriel, still living in North Dakota, keeps in contact with Abe often by phone. He is almost fifty years old with children and grandchildren of his own, so he doesn't often see his dad or half-sisters in St. Paul. Contact with Rebecca's son, Andrew, unfortunately, has been totally lost.

A core character in the Abe Watson story has not yet been described. In some ways, Candace Robinson was a lifesaver for Abe. Unlike Abe, Candace's family has a long history in the US. Her photo album has a picture of her great-great-great-grandmother, Jane Moore, who was born in 1828 and was a slave on a plantation in Durant, Mississippi. Candace easily identifies nine generations in America. Her mother was from Waterloo, Iowa, which she called "Mississippi-moved-north," because the lifestyle was not much different, outhouse and all. Her mother was very active in the struggle for equality for African Americans. When Candace was born, the family lived on Central Avenue in the mostly Black Rondo neighborhood of St. Paul. In spite of the family's long history in the US, she still often gets asked about her country of birth.

Candace doesn't call herself an "activist" because it minimizes true activism as she knows it. But she is very mindful that even regular activities can incorporate actions that promote equality and progress for all. For example, she has participated in numerous panels and groups where she was the only Black, often arguing for equity.

Candace Robinson

Candace has three brothers and one sister. One brother, Stacy Robinson, was a wide receiver for the New York Giants when they won two Super Bowls. A recreation field was named after him near Central High School, where he attended. Sadly, he died from multiple myeloma just as the field was being dedicated and where he was scheduled to give an address.[32]

Candace attended the University of Minnesota without knowing exactly what field of study would be best. Her mother had been a social worker but expected much more from Candace. After two years at the university, she left to work at a Black-owned law office. It was a tough job. She did all the support work— preparation of pleadings, briefings, finances and even the office's taxes, but she learned a ton. Then she worked for seven years at an insurance company, Minnesota Mutual, before joining St. Paul College, a part of the Minnesota state college system.

Candace's first jobs there were administrative, and she began as a receptionist. Sometimes Abe and his mates would drop in to see her and "chat her up." Later she supported the Dean of Deaf Education and learned some sign language skills. She then became a transfer and recruiting specialist, visiting local colleges and high schools, and then a student advisor.

About ten years later, Abe and Candace agreed to meet at Champs restaurant for a cup of coffee. "He snuck up from behind that night to say hi," Candace said, "and I remembered him well. We started to see each other after that."

That time period was a difficult one for Abe, a time when any normal person would have been depressed. He had lost his house, his wife, his kids were off on their own, and there was not much union work available due to the recession. But Candace sensed something in Abraham that was valuable and worthwhile. She loved how he cared for his children and had protected and nurtured them. And Abe sensed that, as an educator, Candace was a caring person, one who could help his children in their lives.

She helped Vicky get into a program at Saint Paul College called "The Power of You," providing two years of college tuition-free to high school graduates. She then pointed Nuwoe toward a surgical technology program at Century College. Nuwoe had completed her associate degree and had taken several difficult nursing courses when Candace suggested the surgical technologist program.

In Abraham, Candace saw a man who was funny, hardworking, and who had love for his children, his church, was respectful, and loved life. She also liked his crazy stories and optimism. Some of his Liberian parables she especially likes are:

1. *When you go into a new room, don't hang your hat so high that you can't reach it when you leave.* In other words, stay humble, don't embarrass yourself.

2. *If you sleep any longer, the sun will cook your butt like a pie.* Meaning: Get up! The early bird gets the worm.

3. *Eat corn when your teeth are growing.* This implies that when your teeth fall out, you won't be able to enjoy corn any more—you must do things before it is too late.

4. One Abe's father often used, *No matter how tall you get, I can still bend you*—meaning that a child can never grow so big that their parent can no longer "handle" them.

Candace and Abe were becoming better friends, but nothing serious. When Abe had to move, Candace and her brother found a place for Abe and Vicky to live. Vicky was taking cosmetology classes, but one day, after school closed, she left, beginning a life on her own terms.

After a couple of years, Abe asked Candace about moving in together. He felt he was wasting a lot of money for an apartment of his own. After her initial shock, Candace warmed up to the idea, and they have lived together ever since. They agreed they were too old for a fancy wedding, so they met at city hall and were married in 2018.

They both enjoy their lives together. Candace sometimes teases Abraham, treating him like a child saying, "Did you wash up? Don't forget to eat. Time for bed."

Candace is serious about her work and continues as an administrator at the college. Abe retired from his union electrician jobs in 2019, just before the pandemic hit, which gives him a lot of free time to work in his gardens, fix things at church and make a dozen calls every day to check on friends.

Nijah, Nula and Adrian (in back), Abe, Nuwoe
and Vicky (family photo).

So Abraham's journey pauses here, surrounded by family and dozens of good friends. The little country boy who wore inner-tube shoes while carrying baskets of rice stalks through the forest has found a safe place. He hates that everything in America requires money, even to fish or to get rid of garbage. But it has brought him a life he couldn't have imagined back in Liberia. It's not a carefree life since there is always stress in the US, but it is a good life. What will he do next?

Ron's View

We should start treating immigrants like Abraham as heroes. All his life, he did what was right, regardless of the difficulty. He studied diligently while those around him were finding reasons to drop out.

He stood up with courage and a rock to a teacher who was unfair. He took responsibility for his work and family and directly confronted danger and terror. He survived by creativity and guts when people all around him were being tortured or killed. He saw hatred and corruption for what they were and cared about others. He was smart enough to see reality and brave enough to head to a new world with confidence and goodwill. He adapted to a new reality in the US and emerged as a friend with Christ-like generosity.

How many heroes like Abraham have come to America? How many have brought their will to overcome sacrifice and struggle? Being an immigrant has always been tough, but immigrants and their children and grandchildren enrich America. Why can't we understand this? As this is written, the US has a shortage of workers, and it's hurting the economy. At the same time, immigrants are begging to enter. The multicultural experiment that is America must succeed. It is the path for all countries that care about the future.

So much of human pain is due to our thinking of some people as unimportant or enemies. Almost any reason is enough to belittle someone or consider them the *"other"*—skin color, sex, religion, wealth or lack of wealth, intelligence, politics, immigration status, type of work or lack of work. Over two-thirds of the almost eight billion people in the world are Black or Brown. It is long past time to think of everyone as humans, not as the others.

Endnotes

1   Stephen Ellis, *The Mask of Anarchy: The Destruction of Liberia and the Religious Dimension of an African Civil War*, 2nd edition.

2   J. H. B. Latrobe, *Biography of Elder Lott Cary*.

3   Betty Wood, *The Origins of American Slavery* (Hill and Wang, 1997).

4   Ben Finley, "Virginia marks pivotal moment when African slaves arrived," *Associated Press*, August 22, 2019.

5   Katharine Gerbner, *Christian Slavery: Conversion and Race in the Protestant Atlantic World*.

6   Sheldon Harris, *Paul Cuffe: Black America and the African Return* (New York: Simon and Schuster, 1972).

7   Tom W. Schick, *Behold the Promised Land: A History of Afro-American Settlers in Nineteenth-Century Liberia* (Johns Hopkins University Press).

8   Charles Henry Huberich, *The Political and Legislative History of Liberia*.

9   Schick.

10 Ellis.

11 Ibid.

12 Thomas Pakenham, *The Scramble for Africa: White Man's Conquest of the Dark Continent from 1876 to 1912*.

13 Finley.

14 Thomas Roberts, *Area Handbook for Liberia*.

15 René Otayek, *Encyclopédie Universalis*, Libéria, 1999 Edition.

16 Richard Tolbert, "Liberia: William R. Tolbert – 'In the Pantheon of Great African Leaders,'" *allAfrica*, https://allafrica.com/stories/200905280621.html.

17 Blaine Harden, "Candidate Doe Allows Election," *The Washington Post*, October 16, 1985.

18 Alan Heil, *Voice of America: A History* (Columbia University Press, 2003).

19 "Charles Taylor Fast Facts," *CNN*, January 17, 2022, https://cnn.it/3jhgkvc.

20 Steven Ellis, *The Mask of Anarchy*, 2nd edition, (New York University Press, 2005), 78.

21 Ibid., 79.

22 Ibid., 112.

23 Stephan Faris, "Welcoming America With Loaded Arms," *Time*, July 14, 2003.

24 Ellis, 5–11.

25 Coercion and Intimidation of Child Soldiers to Participate in Violence," *Human Rights Watch*, April 16, 2008, no. 1, https://bit.ly/37cRfiC.

26 David Leveill, "A new investigation into Firestone's rubber plantation sheds light on Liberia's civil war," *PRI*, November 18, 2014, https://bit.ly/35XBBqS.

27 Ellis, 148–149.

28 Kylin Navarro, "Liberian Women Act to End Civil War," *Global Nonviolent Action Database*, October 2010, https://bit.ly/3rjxDAh.

29 "Education," US Agency for International Development, July 2021, https://www.usaid.gov/liberia/education.

30 International Institute of Minnesota, Minnesota's Refugee and Immigrant Population, Liberia, https://bit.ly/3LS4V1m.

31 Jim Walsh, "'A Phenomenal Moment': Minnesota Liberians Celebrate Their Hard-won Path to US Citizenship," *MINNPOST*, January 6, 2020, https://bit.ly/3rjHC8N.

32 Frederick Melo, "NFL's Stacy Robinson to be Remembered at Rec Center Reopening," *St. Paul Pioneer Press*, May 17, 2012, https://bit.ly/3Jwhg9N.

Acknowledgments

First, I need to thank members of the Watson family—especially Nuwoe, Gabriel, Candice, and of course Abraham for helping to unfold their amazing journey. In particular, Abe has endured endless hours of interviews and questions. It has been our joint labor of love to capture a life so different from my own, and so interesting and meaningful.

My appreciation also to my friend Anshawn Davis for his insights about Liberia and details about his trip back to Liberia with Abraham in 2011.

I make so many errors in life and in my writing that editors like my wife Miriam, my professional friend Pat Morris, and the people at Calumet Editions are essential and greatly appreciated. Thank you, all.

About the Author

Ronald E. Peterson (photo by Erik Saulitus,
Danceprint Studios)

Ron's young life as an emerging nerd/adventurer led him to Caltech, where he roomed with a future Nobel Prize winner, then the University of Illinois at Urbana-Champaign, where he built research refrigerators (good to minus 459.64 degrees Fahrenheit) and received his PhD. in physics. Hired by Honeywell, he worked on solar energy, satellite protection from lasers, and paint coatings. After eight promotions he was responsible for multiple research labs, businesses turning over $200 million per year, and the future technology of the corporation.

None of those experiences prepared him to be a lobbyist, community organizer, teacher, or writer, but that's why retirement has been fun. Like Abraham Watson's life, there were a series of short upheavals, new experiences, and always continual learning. His first book was a memoir called *An Introvert Learns to Fly*. Then, he completed a ten-year project, his second book, *Gardeners of the Universe*, an award winning sci-fi adventure about the next seventy years, replete with aliens, cyber/bio warfare, and the rapid evolution about what it means to be a human. In his spare time he travels, manages a community garden for about two hundred immigrants and teaches high school and college subjects to his five- to fifteen-year-old grandchildren. Through it all his wife Miriam tries to keep his feet on the ground while his head remains affixed in the stars.